A South African
Censor's Tale

To Jane, with compliments
Ars Longa Vita Brevis !

A SOUTH AFRICAN CENSOR'S TALE

Kobus van Rooyen

With a preface by André Brink
and sketches by Marinus Wiechers

Kobus van Rooyen
London 23/11/2011

Protea Book House

Pretoria

2011

A South African Censor's Tale
Kobus van Rooyen

First edition, first impression in 2011 by Protea Book House

PO Box 35110, Menlo Park, 0102
1067 Burnett Street, Hatfield, Pretoria
8 Minni Street, Clydesdale, Pretoria
protea@intekom.co.za
www.proteaboekhuis.com

EDITOR: Danél Hanekom
PROOFREADER: Carmen Hansen-Kruger
ILLUSTRATIONS: Marinus Wiechers
COVER DESIGN: Hanli Deysel
TYPOGRAPHY: 12 on 18 pt Bembo by Hanli Deysel
PRINTED AND BOUND: Creda, Cape Town

CONTENTS

Dedicated to those who have suffered
under the hand of censorship

PREFACE
André Brink

CENSORSHIP IS NOT ONLY AN UNDERSTANDABLE, but a wholly una-voidable attribute of any régime that tends towards the totalitarian – most particularly when, for whatever reason, that régime feels itself threatened. In South Africa, censorship was not high on the priority list for the new Nationalist government that introduced apartheid when it came to power in 1948. This was not because it did not feel threatened, but simply because it perceived other threats as more urgent. Ever since the first movement to promote Afrikaans literature became active late in the nineteenth century, writing in this language remained for a long time closely allied to programmes of Afrikaner political consciousness and nation-building. As more individualist tendencies began to manifest themselves in literature, particularly from the thirties onwards, these occurred mainly in poetry rather than in fiction or drama, and so hardly ever gathered the kind of weight that influences thinking – let alone determines policy – at the national, political level.

But from the mid-1950s it became apparent that Afrikaans literature was developing modes of expression independent of – and at times even hostile to – the political and ideological thinking of the new régime. It was no longer possible for the authorities to take for granted the unquestioning support of writers and other cultural workers, and the same kind of rift was becoming obvious between writing and religion. Nationalist policies in the country had always heavily depended on the support of the Afrikaans Reformed Churches, and the questioning of religious doctrine, even if only by implication, was seen to threaten the political authority of the state as well.

It should not have come as a surprise then when early in the sixties the government started moving emphatically towards new forms of cultural control. Initially at least, it had to move cautiously, attempting to offend or alienate neither its traditional support base of conservative, church-going Afrikaners, nor an increasingly visible younger generation eager to explore and appropriate at least some of the international trends that followed in the wake of World War II. If the government had to make a choice, there was no doubt that it would opt for their traditional rightist support base; but for the time being they tried to walk a tightrope between the extremes. However, such a tightrope required more skill and balancing than this unwieldy establishment could maintain. And after an initial phase, when publications control was entrusted to a widely respected literary man, Prof. Gerrit Dekker, the power in this domain was transferred to a career journalist with an unillustrious career, Mr Jannie Kruger who in my opinion was, quite simply, a fool. The move demonstrated one of the basic weaknesses of the system: the ultimately subjective basis of censorship.

Under Dekker, at least, Afrikaans literature was still "safe". It belonged to the Afrikaner family. What happened to English, was nobody's business. (Even before the Censorship Act was introduced, its godfather in parliament, the unlamented Dr Abraham Jonker, had stated publicly that even Shakespeare could well do with some pruning. He was less forthcoming when asked about whether the

Act would not also jeopardise the Bible.) But with Kruger at the helm, fools were indeed free to rush in where angels had been reluctant to tread. Once the initial hesitation about acting against their "own" had been overcome, the hunt was open. I had the dubious distinction of seeing my novel *Kennis van die Aand* (*Looking on Darkness*) pounced on as the first Afrikaans work of fiction to be banned, and of following the censorship process from the inside.

This included the curious discovery that, after the Board had decided to ban the book but before the decision could be published in the *Government Gazette*, I was not allowed to know the outcome. (A piece of information which was at that juncture particularly vital, as the publisher was anxious to reprint, a costly business he dared not contemplate unless he knew that the new edition could be sold.) When I explained the dilemma to Mr Kruger, he very helpfully suggested that I should lay a charge against my own book, since in that case, as a complainant, I would have a right to know. Such petty actions and decisions became part and parcel of the system.

And when the system was overhauled by a new Act in 1974, a step in which the later State President F.W. de Klerk played an active role, the machinations of censorship became steadily more pernicious and destructive. In the hands of Judge Lammie Snyman the causes of extreme Nationalism and fundamentalist religion were well served, but literature suffered. The infamous *Jakobsen's Index* of banned publications, including hundreds of the greatest titles of world literature, was expanded to well over twenty thousand titles.

The fatal step was taken with the banning of one of the most brilliant novels in Afrikaans, *Magersfontein, O Magersfontein!* by Etienne Leroux, acknowledged even by staunch traditionalists as a masterpiece (and in due course awarded the most prestigious accolade of the Afrikaans Academy, the Hertzog Prize). This was accompanied, almost simultaneously, by the banning of Nadine Gordimer's magnificent *Burger's Daughter*. (But of course, in the eyes of the beholding censors, Gordimer was "merely" an English writer, whereas Leroux, the son of a former Nationalist cabinet minister, came from the front ranks of the "Boer aristocracy".) Clearly, such an outrage could not be tolerated. After the innovative "new literature" of the younger generation, which had dominated the headlines for a decade and which had, in the process, become a litmus test for *political* divisions, the bell was now tolling for censorship in South Africa. For years, the crucial political demarcation between "verligte" (enlightened) and "verkrampte" (narrow-minded) attitudes within the electorate had been predicated, in the first place, on support for, or resistance against, attitudes for and against the literary movement of the so-called "Sestigers".

But now the gloves were off. Naked politics took over.

This came at a moment when literature was, in any case, moving out of the spotlight: by the beginning of the eighties, the government felt threatened more urgently and immediately by agitation in the churches and on the campuses of the country, by newly established trade unions, by threats of international sanctions, by a new United Democratic Front of contestation and resistance within the country, than by literature. This may have made it somewhat easier for the government to back down in the battle against authors and academics. Even so, it took courage to take this gap and start overhauling the system of censorship. Under Snyman this would have been unthinkable: I believe that the man was not even aware of the real issues at stake. And it took his young successor, Kobus van Rooyen, to read the situation lucidly and with a level head, and set in motion a process which would eventually remove the stain of shame the system had left on the arts. This book is, essentially, an account of the battle that had to be waged to recover the self-respect of the nation in the field of culture.

At the time, I was not an unqualified supporter of Kobus van Rooyen. In those days I favoured, uncompromisingly, the approach of direct confrontation. But Van Rooyen, who brought to his task both an acute legal mind and a passion for the arts, believed that this was one war which could be won only from the inside, using the weapons the system itself had placed at his disposal, together with the formidable weight of logic, common sense, understanding, good humour, and tireless persistence.

Today even those of us who once felt ashamed at the very idea of "working within the system" cannot but admire what Van Rooyen has achieved – at a high personal price, and in the face of pig-headed resistance by die-hards from the *ancien régime*, disgraceful attempts to thwart progress, and the weight of sheer stupidity – in order to bring the new South Africa in line with established principles and practices in the rest of the enlightened world; and in line, it should be emphasised, with the requirements of its own constitution.

If there is one depressing note in the text, it is Van Rooyen's warnings against tendencies in the present government's attitudes towards control and censorship which threaten an erosion of the dearly won new freedom and enlightenment, and a return to the mentalities of the *ancien régime*. Against the background of his extensive experience and the clarity of his own insights, these are warnings to be heeded. This long road to yet another form of freedom comes at an important juncture in our post-apartheid history, which serves as an urgent reminder to all those who may have been tempted to think that, our freedom secured, we can now rest on our laurels. The things that are really worthwhile, Goethe already pointed out, are those we have to continue fighting for every day of our lives.

ANDRÉ BRINK

INTRODUCTION

ONE OF THE OBJECTIVES OF THE NATIONAL PARTY, which came into power in South Africa in 1948, was to protect and further Christian morality which, disgracefully, included racial segregation called apartheid. The Afrikaans Reformed Churches supported the system of apartheid and would often remind government that it called itself a "Christian Government" and, accordingly, demanded strict moral and religious censorship from Government. When, in the sixties, Afrikaans authors began describing sex scenes and using crude language in novels, there was grave concern.

A Commission of Inquiry in the fifties had already proposed a system according to which the indecency of publications and films would be regulated by a Board. This Board was established in 1963. Publications were in principle not subjected to pre-control, but were dealt with after complaints from the public, the Police and Customs. However, future issues of publications could also be banned. All films destined to be screened in public were required to be certified by a Board. In the case of publications (which excluded newspapers belonging to Newspaper Press Union members) there would be an appeal to the Supreme Court whilst, in the case of films, there would be an appeal to the Minister of Home Affairs.

As a result of the clash between the approach of the Courts and that of the Board as regards to indecency, especially in publications such as *Scope*, Parliament decided to set up a Publications Appeal Board in 1974. A new Act was passed. At the first level there were committees appointed by the Directorate of Publications. The Board would hear all appeals and its decision on the merits would be final. The recourse to the Courts was limited to a review by three judges.

This book aims to describe the different stages that the new 1974 Appeal Board went through. Except for Chapters 13 and 14, it is intended to be a light and hopefully at times slightly humorous read, and not an academic work.

I have used the term "decadent" to describe the utter disgust with which moralists regarded anything in films and books – especially sex and crude language – which departed from moral ideals, often based on religious norms. In essence this meant that a book or film was not permitted to describe sin. And if sin was referred to, it had to be explicitly rejected as evil. Even that description had to be expressed in vague terms and crude language might possibly, at the worst, have included a word such as "damn it".

My special thanks to Nicol Stassen who was willing to publish this book, Juliette Grosskopf, my daughter, and my wife, Martha, who helped and advised me on the script, and retired Judge of Appeal John Trengove who read the manuscript critically. My editor, Danél Hanekom, has improved this book immensely; for this I am more than grateful! I am grateful to Hanli Deysel for her creative energy with the cover design and layout and to Carmen Hansen-Kruger for her meticulousness during proofreading. My friend of almost fifty years, Prof. Marinus Wiechers, has assisted in making this book a lighter read with his tongue-in-cheek sketches.

I wish to express my gratitude to the Alexander von Humboldt Stiftung, Germany for having supported my research at the Max-

Planck-Institut für ausländisches und internationales Strafrecht in Freiburg im Bresgau. The guidance of Prof. Dr Albin Eser on the relationship between art and law in German legislation proved invaluable. I am also grateful to Prof. Dr Joachim Hermann at the University of Augsburg for his helpful contribution on the way child pornography is dealt with in German law.

Ultimately, my gratitude goes to my wife Martha and my children, Kona, Juliette and Cobus, who watched and waited patiently while I wrote a multitude of judgments in my study over the past thirty years, either as chairman of the Publications Appeal Board (1980–1990), the Press Council (1991–1997), the Broadcasting Complaints Commission (1993–) or as an Acting Judge (2003– 2009) for almost twelve Court terms.

KOBUS VAN ROOYEN
APRIL 2011

ONE
Moral clampdown
1963–1975

WHEN THE NATIONAL PARTY gained control of Parliament in 1948, a paradigm shift in terms of policy took place: the holism of the previous Prime Minister, the world-renowned and respected General Jan Smuts, was replaced by Afrikaner Nationalism. Inspired by National Socialism and Christian principles (often perceived from a political angle), the ideal of the Nationalists was to once again build a nation where Calvinistic principles would reign supreme and South Africa would recapture the essence of the nineteenth-century Republics of the Orange Free State and Transvaal, thereby re-establishing the supremacy of the white Afrikaner. In short, apartheid would lie at the heart of the new government policy, which was, unjustifiably, claimed to be based on biblical principles. The larger white Afrikaans churches supported the government in these claims. Although South Africa was constitutionally not a theocracy, the government often fell back on what it perceived to be Christian principles in support of political and social plans.

The government set about legalising apartheid and some of the first steps taken were criminalising communism;* removing people of colour from the common voters' roll; declaring marriages, sex

---

*   Suppression of Communism Act (No. 44 of 1950).

and sexual immorality between blacks and whites a crime;* isolating black and white people from one another by prohibiting racially mixed living areas; and ensuring that education would be based on Christian national principles. Legislation was also passed to ensure that those publications, films and public entertainment which were deemed to be offensive, indecent, obscene or harmful to public morals, or blasphemous or offensive to religious convictions of a section of the population, would be subject to control by a Publications Board as from 1963.† Included was the prohibition of that which was thought to be in contempt of or ridiculed a section of the population, that which harmed race relations, and finally, material that amounted to be a risk to state security and public order. A Board applied this legislation and when its decisions were not abided by, prosecutions could follow. In the case of publications there was an appeal to the Courts and in the case of films, an appeal to the Minister of Home Affairs. Further legislation made the possession of indecent or obscene photographs and films a crime.‡

The Act of 1963 should be seen against the backdrop of 1962 legislation which made detention without trial possible for a maximum of 90 days, which was later to become 180 days. The new legislation gave the government the opportunity to put authors who attacked the system behind bars and of course to clamp down on freedom of speech, which was part of our common law. The Suppression of Communism Act made it illegal to quote persons listed by the Minister of Justice. The distribution of works that promoted communism was also an offence.

---

*   Sexual Offences Act (No. 23 of 1957).
†   Publications and Entertainments Act (No. 26 of 1963).
‡   The Indecent or Obscene Photographic Matter Act (No. 37 of 1967).

"Communism" was defined widely. The distribution of the works of Marx, Engels, Trotsky and Stalin, to name but a few, were as a result banned and would only, with special permission, be available in a few public and university libraries. The ideal was so strong and the officials at Customs so ill-informed that it is true that the books *Black Beauty* and *Anna Karenina* were seized by Customs; in the case of *Black Beauty* for obvious racist reasons and in the case of *Anna Karenina*, because it was thought to promote communism. It is also not apocryphal that copies of Michelangelo's *David* were covered at the one strategic spot which must have led to the fall of Bathsheba. The concept of a unitary democratic state where black and white could vote was an abomination to this new government and its legislation.

Prof. Gerrit Dekker, a well-known literary expert from the University of Potchefstroom, was appointed as the first chairman of the Publications Board in 1963. The new Board demonstrated its first signs of ultra-conservatism when it banned Wilbur Smith's *When the Lion Feeds* in 1965. The Appellate Division of the Supreme Court confirmed this ban.* Judge of Appeal Frans Rumpff filed a famous dissenting† judgment. I remember how, as a law student in 1965, I had, with many others who had suddenly shown an interest

---

*   *Publications Control Board v William Heinemann Ltd and Others* 1965(4) SA 137(A).

†   A "dissenting (or minority) judgment" is where a conclusion different from the conclusion reached by the majority of Judges is reached by a single Judge or a minority of the Judges. The decision of the latter is not that of the Court, which is represented by the majority of Judges. Obviously the Court's decision is the final decision. Yet, minority opinions have, all over the world, at times, been accepted by a Court and, in that sense, have been proved to have been correct. The majority judgment is the judgment of the Court and constitutes the order of the Court.

in the law reports in the law library, read snippets from the book as quoted by Appeal Judge Rumpff in his judgment. Since the book was banned, this was the only spot where one could read parts of the book. Even in those very conservative times the ban was not justified. The sex scenes referred to in the banning judgment simply disappeared in the light of the whole and were, in any case, not even remotely explicit in themselves. The ban on the book amounted to nothing else than an application of what is called the isolated-passage approach to censorship, where the consideration of context is irrelevant.

No historical look at censorship would be complete without a reference to that famous, or infamous, biweekly magazine, *Scope*. It published what the Board called "lust-provoking and provocative photographs" of attractive women and the cardinal question was whether the material was calculated to excite lust in the minds of reasonable men and teenagers. By the time *Scope* appeared on the market, Prof. Dekker had been succeeded full time by Jannie Kruger, who was ridiculed by newspapers and their cartoonists as the epitome of conservative Calvinistic principles. The famous tug-of-war between the Supreme Court and the Board related to the numerous instances when the Board would, between 1967 and 1974, ban the distribution of *Scope* with its semi-nudes* and the Supreme Court would lift the ban a few hours or a day later. Of course, this only led to the soaring of the sales of *Scope*. I do not believe that it is apocryphal that thousands of men would ensure that they had already purchased their copies before 13:00 on a Friday when the *Government Gazette*, with the regular ban on distribution, would

---

*   That is, no female nipples, genitalia or pubis could be seen.

appear. Married men would, it was whispered, keep their copy of *Scope* at their offices or in their briefcases and many of them would argue in their defence that they bought *Scope* for its interesting articles. *Playboy, Penthouse* and *Hustler* magazines were permanently on the list of banned magazines. The Afrikaans churches and Action Moral Standards were raging at *Scope* and the "sinful lust" which it was pumping into the community. Naturally, the sales of the magazine soared with this publicity …

When the appeal to the Courts was substituted by an appeal to the Publications Appeal Board, one of the reasons put forward in Parliament was the disrupting effect of the constant setting aside by the Courts of the Board's orders in regard to *Scope*. There was obviously a clear rift between the judicial view of indecency and what the conservative Board regarded as indecent.

Customs and Excise and the Security Police ensured that all publications which would even remotely propagate or incline towards a new democratic state were brought to the attention of the Board. Such publications were summarily banned and placed on a list that was published in the *Government Gazette*. The Act of 1963 did not provide for a possession ban. However, the possession of indecent photographs and films was an offence in terms of the Indecent or Obscene Photographic Matter Act of 1967. A general possession ban would be made possible by the Act of 1974.

During this period a group of Afrikaans authors, known as the "Sestigers",* began writing in much more realistic terms. Sexuality and crude and profane language suddenly entered the scene. Books such as *Lobola vir die Lewe* by André P. Brink and *Sewe Dae by die*

---

*   Which means that they were writing in the sixties.

Silbersteins by Etienne Leroux were vehemently attacked by the conservative sector of the public. The article about a female reader who had said in her complaint to the Publications Board that she had become sexually aroused sixty-nine times while reading Leroux's book, made it to "page three" in many newspapers. I was rather surprised at this claim. I was a student at the time and I recall how I smuggled the *Silbersteins* into our home and read it cover to cover in one night – finding nothing which was even remotely lustful or even explicit in the book. Afrikaans church leaders expressed their shock and put pressure on the government to clamp down on these authors. Of course, *Lady Chatterley's Lover*, which had already by 1961 been found not to be indecent by juries in the UK and the USA, remained solidly banned in South Africa.

The heat was still on by 1975 when the new Publications Appeal Board was appointed to replace the Minister and the Courts as a body of appeal. The message which we gleaned from newspaper reports as to what Government had planned with this new legislation was, *inter alia*, to "cleanse" literature from its "dirty-mouthed" South African authors.

In 1974 the Publications Board banned its first Afrikaans book, André P. Brink's *Kennis van die Aand*, translated into English as *Looking on Darkness*. The publishers appealed and the Full Bench of the Cape Supreme Court heard the matter. Brink had realistically described the harrowing experience of a coloured actor with the Security Police under the apartheid laws. The protagonist, Joseph Malan, had fallen in love with a white woman and had a passionate sexual relationship with her. The relationship was prohibited under the segregation laws of the apartheid regime. Their sex was described quite explicitly for those times. Particularly problematic (for some conservative readers) was the parallel which Brink drew between the suffering of Christ and the suffering of Joseph Malan. The "cross" for Joseph Malan was the ban on sex between whites and blacks and his suffering on that apartheid "cross". The novel also contained profane language and in one scene, where Joseph has sex with a prostitute in Amsterdam, she exclaims "Jesus" when she urgently invites him to have sex with her – sex being described by way of a crude Afrikaans term comparable to the intercourse language of the gamekeeper in *Lady Chatterley's Lover*. Three Judges of the Supreme Court unanimously held that the book was offensive to the religious convictions of the Christian section of the South African populace as a result of descriptions in the novel that amounted to "a crude mixture of sex and religion".*

The approach of the new 1975 Appeal Board was as conservative as the old 1963 Board's approach, although I believe that the old Board, with Prof. Gerrit Dekker as its chairperson, would not have banned *Magersfontein, O Magersfontein!* No literary expert would ever have banned a masterpiece such as *Magersfontein, O Magersfontein!* When Jannie Kruger took over as chairman later in the 1960s, the approach became much more conservative and I believe that the Board would have banned *Magersfontein, O Magersfontein!*, as had been the case with *Kennis van die Aand* † in 1974. Works such as *Lady Chatterley's Lover* had already been banned and Jack Cope's *The Dawn Comes Twice*, an innocuous work in which the apartheid police was shown to act brutally, was banned after 1975 when the new Act of 1974 came into effect.

★   *Buren Uitgewers (Edms) Bpk en 'n ander Raad van Beheer oor Publikasies* 1975(1) SA 379(C).

†   *Looking on Darkness.*

In 1974 the celebrated stage entertainers, Des and Dawn Lindberg, produced the play *Godspell*. Complaints were received and the Board banned the play. At the heart of the ban lay the accusation that the play did not conform to the rendition of Jesus's life as described in the Gospel. The Lindbergs lodged an urgent appeal to the Supreme Court and Judge Lammie Snyman,* from the Witwatersrand Local Division of the Supreme Court, heard the appeal. Judge Snyman upheld the appeal and ordered a few minor amendments. This amounted to an enlightened approach and was praised in the media and entertainment circles. Dawn Lindberg later told me that the revisions could not, in practice, be made and that they continued with the play without any changes.

By 1969 *Jesus Christ Superstar* had made its way onto the London stage. This musical, as is well known, portrays the passion of Jesus in a rock opera. The Director-General of the South African Broadcasting Corporation, Douglas Fuchs, authorised a single broadcast of the lyrics on the English radio service on 31 March 1971. Immediately after the broadcast, strong protests were received from many cultural organisations, ecclesiastical quarters and individual listeners. The Board of the Corporation decided that there would be no further broadcasts of this record. The complaint was that the lyrics portrayed Jesus, enacted by a "sinful" human being who was also a rock star, in a manner which conflicted with the Gospel. The lyrics also, it was said, implied that there was a sexual relationship between Mary Magdalene and Jesus.

Subsequently, the Publications Board also received complaints

---

* Judge Snyman was to become the first chairman of the Publications Appeal Board in 1975.

and the record was banned as being offensive to the religious convictions of Christians. The distributors of the record appealed to the Durban and Coast Local Division High Court, Justice Milne presiding. The appeal was upheld and the decision of the Board set aside. By consent the Board then appealed directly to the Appellate Division in Bloemfontein. The Appellate Division upheld the appeal and confirmed the ban on the distribution of the record. It ruled that the manner in which the life of Jesus was portrayed, was offensive to Christians. The lyrics were not compatible with the dignity of Jesus as portrayed in the Gospel. In the light of this approach by the Court, Chief Justice Rumpff held that it was unnecessary to decide whether the lyrics were also blasphemous.*

IN 1972 THE CNA (CENTRAL NEWS AGENCY) planned to distribute the booklet *Naked Yoga*. It contained nude poses by women illustrating a variety of yoga positions. Customs and Excise referred the matter to the Board, which held that the publication was intended for the advancement of the practice and teaching of yoga and that it was therefore exempted from control. In terms of the amended Act, the Minister of Home Affairs, however, ordered the Board to reconsider its decision. The Board then revoked its previous decision. The CNA lodged an appeal to the Cape Supreme Court, arguing that the booklet was not indecent or obscene. The Court held that the publication was exempted by the Act. The Board then appealed to the Appellate Division. Two appeal judges held that the work was not exempted by the Act and that the nude poses were

---

*   *Publications Control Board v Gallo (Africa) Ltd* 1975(3) SA 665(A).

indecent or obscene. However, the majority of the Court held the publication to be exempted by the Act because it was a scientific publication.*

There was an outcry from conservative circles. The nudity of the models demonstrating the yoga positions was regarded as being at the heart of decadent conduct. Minister Connie Mulder also did not agree with the Appeal Court's majority judgment and simply removed the possibility for such a finding in future by convincing Parliament to repeal the exemptions. This is a good example of how the National Party played for the gallery of the conservative vote. The 1994 Ministerial Task Group, which I chaired, re-introduced the exemptions for the new Films and Publications Act of 1996. That such exemptions are constitutionally justified and necessary are clear from the judgment of the 2003 Constitutional Court in *De Reuck v Director of Public Prosecutions WLD and Others*.† However, from 1999 to 2009 Parliament seemingly ignored the Court's ruling and, currently, no exemptions are provided for in the case of child pornography. A clear overkill, which I will discuss in Chapter 13.

UNDER THE NATIONALIST GOVERNMENT, the Board had to certify in advance all films that were destined for public screening. Since the test lay in the nature of the film, it was also not permissible to screen such a film in a private place. In other words, only home movies were exempted from certification. Nudity and sex were

---

*   *Publications Control Board v Central News Agency Ltd* 1977(1) SA 717(A).
†   2004(1) SA 406(CC).

ordered to be excised, and crude language – everything from "shit" to "fuck" – was also cut. Any film portraying racial integration was either banned or cut where relevant. Of course, the possession of any film that included sexual indecency was prohibited in terms of the Indecent or Obscene Photographic Matter Act of 1967, whether it was home-made or not.

It was possible to appeal to the Minister of Home Affairs against decisions of the Board on films. The Minister was known to invite members of the public to watch the films with him and he obviously asked their opinions. Since he was supposed to have made up his mind on his own accord, I have little doubt that this procedure was irregular. However, film distributors never challenged him on this aspect. At least one of these appeals drew a few laughs from the enlightened section of the community. A local production, *Debbie,* by Tommie Meyer portrayed the plight of a young student, Debbie, who fell pregnant. The film effectively portrayed the problems she had with her parents, the community and her church minister. The Board imposed a 4 to 12 age restriction on the film. On appeal by Tommie Meyer to have the age restriction reduced, he found to his astonishment that Deputy Minister Viljoen had increased the age restriction to 21! It is to the credit of Mrs Johanna Raath, chairperson of the Women's Federation at the time, who approached the Minister and convinced him to reinstate the age restriction of 12. I later watched this film in the late 1990s on the subscription broadcaster, DSTV. It was broadcast on a Sunday afternoon without any age restriction! That anyone could have regarded an age restriction as necessary for this innocuous film astounded me.

But the sixties and the seventies were very conservative times in South Africa, which even allowed for a morally and religiously inspired book-burning at times. It is a known fact that in the seventies several books were burnt at the town centre of a small town in the western Transvaal. But of course, as Freud observed after the Nazis burnt his books: there is some improvement; earlier the people would have burnt him! Even today in the twenty-first century, the Broadcasting Complaints Commission constantly receives complaints from the public on the very same kind of matters: crude and profane language, sex and nudity and the like.

Moral outrage at crudities in plays and the cinema was not limited to South Africa. When Seán O'Casey's play, *The Plough and the Stars* (1924), was performed in Dublin's Abbey Theatre, a riot broke out in the theatre, amongst other things as a result of the opinion that the play amounted to an attack on the men in the uprising against England and the inclusion of a prostitute in Act 2.* O'Casey went on to become a world-famous playwright. And of course, Molière's brilliant satirical plays evoked political, religious and moral wrath amongst his seventeenth-century contemporaries. Fortunately, he had the protection of the King! In Shakespeare's sixteenth century, the actors of the *Isle of Dogs* were in fact imprisoned for a time for having taken part in a play at *The Swan* – the play having been regarded as scandalous by the authorities.† And then, of course, there was the famous Alfred Jarry play, *Ubu Roi*, in which Jarry showed no respect for royalty or society, provoking the audience from the very first word with his wordplay. In 1896, the play opened in Paris with the exclamation "Merdre". The word, a bastardised version of the word "merde", means "shit". The audience, as it were, attacked

---

*   See the 1965 film *Young Cassidy* directed by Jack Cardiff.
†   See Shapiro, *1599: A Year in the life of William Shakespeare* (Faber and Faber, 2005) 14.

the stage and the play was halted. The next evening the play again commenced with "Merdre" and once again the stage was attacked by the audience … As a result, the play was banned and Jarry replaced it with a puppet show with the same characters and text. I need not say more. Moral wrath at a word which was not that uncommon in ordinary life went overboard when it was repeated on stage. And thereby the brilliant burlesque and wordplay of the play was lost to audiences of the time.

One could hardly believe that half a century later South Africa had its own peculiar moral riots. "Riots" that consisted of the urge to ban anything which did not accord with the perception of Afrikaner moral and religious values as inspired by Calvinistic views of what is virtuous and good. No crude or profane words or sex in novels; no nudity or inviting sexual poses in magazine and, even, no mixed swimming in the nude as described in one book; and yes, no interracial sex. This all amounted to an overkill which led to a backlash, which is described in the next few chapters.

TWO

First steps
1975–1977

THE FIRST APPEAL BOARD had hardly been constituted under the Act of 1974 when it was put to the test in April 1975. *Brandwag*, a popular Afrikaans magazine, published all previously banned photographs, which included a semi-nude photo of a famous local entertainer, Glenda Kemp, with her pet python.

The Appeal Board confirmed the ban of nudity displaying female breasts, despite hopes that the new Board would be more tolerant of nudity in magazines. The emphasis was placed on Christian values which were ordained to be applicable in terms of section 1 of the new Act. Even nudes of Toulouse Lautrec and Ingres were included in the ban since they, according to the Appeal Board, were published "out of context" in this popular magazine. The same results followed as regards *Scope* for scantily clad models, where their poses were seen as aimed at exciting lust – defined widely. On the lighter side: our typist was not *au fait* with art and when I dictated the name of Toulouse Lautrec, she typed "Too Loose the Track"!

How loose the tracks would get in later years was quite unbelievable, compared to those stifling pre-1980 times. Only one upside-down phallus by Hieronymus Bosch on the cover of a gramophone record cover made it through the eye of the needle. Appeal

Board member, Prof. Grové, was quick to recognise the typical style of the famous Dutch artist.

By the end of November 1975, Dr Connie Mulder, Minister of Home Affairs, issued a statement that censorship was to become stricter. This led to fears that literature would also be judged even stricter than under the Publications and Entertainments Act of 1963 which led to the ban on André P. Brink's *Kennis van die Aand*. Koos Human from Human & Rousseau confirmed that, for the first time, a manuscript was rejected for fear that it might be banned. It would simply be too costly to publish an Afrikaans translation of André Brink's *A Moment in the Wind*. As matters turned out, the Afrikaans book was published and not banned.

That the rules were stricter though, was illustrated by the banning of *A Sparrow Falls* by Wilbur Smith in 1977 as a result of a non-explicit sex scene in a library. The Appeal Board had requested a professor in Afrikaans literature, T.T. Cloete, to give his opinion as to whether the scene was indecent. The answer was in the affirmative. I voted against the ban. I had the impression that according to some literary critics of the time, sex scenes should be limited to works of exceptional literary merit. This could, to my mind, simply not be the case. The question was one of indecency or obscenity and any text should be judged within the appropriate context, even a scene in a book that was a mere potboiler. Of course, *A Sparrow Falls* was much more than a potboiler. The library sequence in the novel was simply not that explicit to be regarded as of such a nature that it could be banned as a result of this scene. This approach amounted to nothing else than an application of the isolated-passage approach which was attributed to Chief Justice Steyn as a result of his judgment on *When the Lion Feeds*. To my mind, the sexuality in a work would have to be predominantly explicit and without any function other than to describe such sexuality, before indecency could be found. In any case, the words "indecency", "obscenity" and "offensiveness" are so vague that they simply cannot and should not be used as criteria under a constitutional dispensation.

FINALLY, BY 1994 WHEN WE DRAFTED the new Films and Publications Act, my view on what was unacceptable had changed completely: I was of the opinion that only hard pornography in visual form was unacceptable. Soft pornography in visual form would be available in licensed premises and, elsewhere, classification and age restrictions would take care of the balance.

The vague terms "indecent", "obscene" and "offensive" were not included in the new Act. Science, art, literature and drama were excluded from any ban. In Chapter 12, I shall discuss what the Task Group advised in this regard.

IN 1976 THE NEW APPEAL BOARD issued a statement that newspapers would be prosecuted if they attempted to influence decisions of the Appeal Board. The new Act indeed protected the Appeal Board against contempt and that included the said rule. It was clear that the censorship machinery was clamping down not only on films and publications under its control, but also, indirectly, on newspapers that were openly showing their disgust at the new, stricter approach. Newspapers that were members of the Newspaper Press Union were of course not subject to the Act themselves. But the Media Council had jurisdiction to hear complaints against these newspapers. Of course, the Media Council could not ban a newspaper, but it could order a correction or an apology.

A book of poems – *Skryt om 'n sinkende skip blou te verf* (1972) – by Breyten Breytenbach, was banned by a Publications Committee in 1975. An appeal was lodged with the Appeal Board. It was a collection of poems which, amongst other things, attacked the Security Police on their actions against the majority of the populace who were not permitted to vote and were even subjected to detention without trial. The booklet included several drawings, some of which might have been indecent in the eye of conservative South Africans, who would, in any case, not have read or bought the collection of poems.

On the day when the matter came before the Appeal Board, the court room was packed with authors and journalists. The interest in the matter was probably intensified as a result of the commencement of the criminal trial against the author, who was accused of treason for his support of the armed struggle against the apartheid regime.

When the case was called, André Brink, the author of *Looking on Darkness*, which had been banned by the Supreme Court in 1974, stood up and announced that Breytenbach had instructed him to withdraw the appeal against the ban. In hindsight, I cannot believe that this was South Africa. The poems would have had a very limited audience and within that sphere the publication could not have posed any risk to the security of the state or the public order.

Interestingly enough, Breytenbach has been awarded the highest South African literary prize, the Hertzog prize, at least three times after 1976. Breytenbach was also awarded the Dutch Van Hoogstraten prize for *Skryt*. The mere fact that *Skryt* was banned by a publications committee is sufficient to justify an outcry of scandalous shame against the South African censorship system at the time.

I FEEL IT IS NECESSARY TO WRITE critically about those times so that those mistakes will never be repeated. Freedom of speech lies at the heart of democracy – a phrase already used in the 1994 report of the Ministerial Task Group. Our task was to advise the new democratic government on a new, constitutionally compatible Films and Publications Act – and it was vital that this Act should not be put at risk by the voice of fundamentalists. Those years were particularly formative for me: to experience the bias of many church leaders and some politicians was a valuable element in the formation of my all-encompassing ideal in the eighties to set South Africa free from those incredible preconceived ideas. The arts, which includes literature and drama, and is a lifeline to an informed society, had to be free. It was my opinion that children could be protected by age restrictions and the classification of films.

IN 1977 I WROTE A DISSENTING OPINION in which I argued that *Scope's* provocative photographs of beautiful young women were not intended to excite lust and that the test was, in any case, too vague and open to subjective decision making. To my surprise, *Rapport*, the Afrikaans Sunday newspaper, got hold of the judgment and the early Sunday morning posters read: "Judge and Professor Clash on Nudes!" Unaware of the posters, I arrived at church that morning – a member of the church council – to find brethren on the council shaking my hand with some unease and a wary look in the eye.

I happened to be in the congregation of one of the leaders in the crusade against nudity. His action group had, in fact, led to the relocation of a 1972 Tienie Pritchard* statue, with its nudes, to the second floor (described as "P" in the lift) veranda *behind* the Civitas Home Affairs Building in Pretoria. The statue had originally been intended for the foyer and was fittingly called "Life Cycle". Senior civil servants, who every day had lunch at an up-market restaurant on the P veranda, walked past the statue with a glance and often a smile in its direction – the lonely, isolated nudes staring into the distance – possibly their "eyes" would have been able to see the Union Buildings, seat of Government. The Union Buildings is not

---

*   Tienie Pritchard has over the years gained international recognition for his work. The statue (1987) in Bedforview, Johannesburg, colloquially called "The Miner", is a splendid example of his work. His website is www.tieniepritchard.co.za.

far from the veranda referred to above. The nudes were clearly now destined only for the view of the few who dined in luxury within a few meters of the sculpture. One wonders what future generations would think of the work of art when excavating Pretoria: was this a South African oracle of Delphi? Or were these real people caught by a South African volcanic eruption and turned into stone? Or was it a latter-day Lot's wife and a few friends who looked back? Unfortunately my futuristic speculation has, as it were, been thwarted by the recent move of the statue to an art gallery at Hartebeespoort, not too far from Pretoria.

IN SO FAR AS FILMS WERE CONCERNED there was also no scope for nudity and crude words. The approach was that if the nudity and crude language were cut, then an age restriction was not really necessary. Ster-Kinekor, a local cinema operator, at one stage, decided to state at the outset that it had agreed to an age restriction and that the age restriction would then counter the need for cuts. But the policy remained intact – cut the scenes and then age restrictions would be redundant. In only one respect did the Appeal Board introduce a more relaxed approach: Eastern kung-fu films. Up to then these type of films had been banned, but since the chairman had knowledge of karate he convinced us that there was no harm in these films; they simply illustrated different poses and did not amount to real violence. We received a letter from a committee member who severely criticised our approach. He was unhappy since we rejected his reasoning on a kung-fu matter. He felt that kung-fu films would fill white South Africans with a fear for the "Chinese danger" and that all these films posed a risk to state security. With respect, an astounding viewpoint. Furthermore, any film in which a black person was at the head of a detective team or charge office was banned since it would be harmful to race relations. I recall how a scene where a white man places his hand on a coloured woman's leg was cut as harmful to race relations! Looking back I can hardly believe that this was policy.

On one occasion even the word "whore" had to be excised from the credits at the end of the film. In Burt Reynolds's *The End,* the word "God", used casually and in moments of comical agony, had to be removed 120 times. More than 180 cuts of the word "fuck" were ordered in regard to the gangster film *Scarface,* in which the accomplished actor, Al Pacino, acted as the gang leader. Merit and functionality were irrelevant and cleaning up movies was the paradigm within which we worked. A member of the public who attended a screening with the permission of the chairperson told me that he counted 120 flashlight moments while he was watching the movie. We would write down all crude words for excision and, of course, a flashlight was necessary for this work … Was this a form of film "torching"? Fortunately, the famous beach kissing scene between Burt Lancaster and Deborah Kerr in *From Here to Eternity* had already been passed in earlier years, or else it might have also been shortened in the conservative seventies.

Of course, it all started when Rhett Butler and Scarlet O'Hara, in the film version of *Gone with the Wind,* had the following parting dialogue:

Scarlet: Where shall I go? What shall I do?

Rhett : Frankly my dear, I don't give a damn (final exit Rhett)

The word "damn" had up to that stage (1938) been objected to by American censors. Shortly before the release of the film, the Production Code was amended to accommodate the word when functionally used. In 2005 the American Film Institute voted the sentence the number one movie line of all times. The rumour at the time that Zanuck had to pay a fine of US$5000 to the Institute seems to be unfounded.

The word "goddamn" in a film was for the first time officially allowed in South Africa in 1980 by the Appeal Board that I chaired. Yet, somehow "damn" was not censored out from the copy of *Gone with the Wind* that I saw as a kid in the Kokstad Town Hall in 1956. Well, of course, the expression "damn it" was often used, even by conservative South Africans. It was not intended as a profanity and has become much more of an exclamation of utter disgust. And so many words crept into the local languages which, on a strict interpretation, were profane. Of course, some Afrikaans-speaking people could hardly speak English in those times. But "dammit" was a word they often used! In fact, I believe that they thought the word was an Afrikaans word. As a kid, I did!

WHILE THE CHAIRMAN OF THE APPEAL BOARD was on leave during December 1976, we approved the film *The Omen*. I acted as chairman. The two co-opted members and I were severely criticised for doing this. The film portrays a young boy, Damien, as the antichrist. Damien has enormous evil powers and ultimately kills his parents in a hair-raising scene. Unbeknown to the Board, the distributors had cut the last part of the film where the US President adopts the boy, who then goes ahead and kills the President as well. In the place of the excised scene the distributors inserted a quote from the book Revelations that evil would ultimately be overcome. This was, I thought, a splendid thriller, not to be taken seriously. Nevertheless, the Directorate was flooded with letters and telegrams. I read one which came from Action Moral Standards: "Dr Mulder, are you still a Christian?" Dr Mulder happened to be the leader of the National Party in conservative Transvaal and it was quite an embarrassment to him as Minister of Home Affairs when we approved the film. He was also tipped to become the next Prime Minister. I happened to be in Cape Town at that time and he invited me to afternoon tea at Parliament where we had an amicable chat. To reach the tearoom we had to move through a barrage of shaking hands – Dr Mulder had just held an inspiring pro-apartheid speech in Parliament. Over tea he said that he understood our decision wholeheartedly, but that I should bear in mind that there was a vociferous "right wing", which could (politically) not be ignored.

To my mind the film was nothing more than a thriller that employed the theme of the antichrist, which was triumphant in this film. I could not believe that anyone would take the film seriously. The two co-opted members on that panel agreed with my view. They were a sociologist, Prof. Jannie Pieterse and a lawyer, Prof. Fanie van Jaarsveld. Dr Mulder had a sharp intellect and a splendid sense of humour. He clearly understood the reason why we had approved the film. However, conservative politics were a concern. Dr Klaas van Wyk de Vries, one of the members of the Appeal Board, phoned me later and told me that he had been to see the film and that it was shockingly offensive. This astounded me. Was there no room for a thriller to employ the antichrist theme? People, to my mind, were simply not so gullible as to take a thriller seriously. It was evident to me that many conservative people do not wish to see the power of evil, even in a fictional thriller.

In 1976 a committee ordered that a scene be excised from a film where a church minister was involved in street preaching. It was argued that a minister of religion, in terms of the Protestant Church procedures, was not permitted to preach unless his church council was present. The role of fiction was totally misunderstood. On appeal we set this decision aside.

THE ROCKY HORROR PICTURE SHOW MADE an unusual entrance into our lives. The film had been passed by a publications committee in 1977. Conservative groupings heard about the decadence portrayed in the film – it is doubtful whether they ever went to see the film and, as it were, "looked at what's on the slab in the lab". The fear was that young men would resort to the kind of dress worn by the main character, Dr Frank-N-Furter. The film also portrayed what the pressure groups regarded to be a degenerate lifestyle because of the young males wearing long female stockings and painting their faces like females in the film. The Minister, who was authorised to refer a film or publication which was not banned by a committee to the Appeal Board, referred the film to us later in 1977 and the Board held it to be harmful - it portrayed the abnormal as normal and natural, satisfying and right. This behaviour was said to fall squarely within the detailed definition of "harmful to public morals" in the Act of 1963 and since the new Act simply prohibited material that was harmful to public morals, the old detailed definition was adopted by the Appeal Board.

This was truly an overkill and in the eighties, under my chairmanship, we approved the film and nobody walked the streets clad in peculiar dress. A few young men turned up in stockings at Rocky Horror parties but, as in the case of partygoers dressed up as Dracula, the make-believe was just for fun and did not gain support or made anyone falter, except in so far as the high heels could have made one stumble! In any case, the morals of the state would not totter, to use a Shakespearean phrase. What is more, in modern society dress has become a matter of individual choice.

Of course, in those stifling times, the Beatles were regarded as taboo to listen to … Had John Lennon not said: "We're bigger than Jesus"? Of course, this was quoted out of context by South African believers and for quite a time the State broadcaster did not broadcast their songs!

Following the ban of *The Rocky Horror Picture Show*, the film distributors decided to boycott the 1975 Appeal Board. Almost no appeals were received from the industry. The appeals were almost solely those of the directorate who appealed against decisions made by committees. Even *Scope*, which published semi-nudes, was quiet for a while. The rumour became a belief – there was no hope on appeal where even more cuts could be added. The addition of more cuts on appeal by a distributor was irregular and I stopped this in 1980.

The press was also becoming increasingly critical of our approach. Journalists were not permitted to attend film viewings and were in the dark as to what we saw in the dark theatres. It was impossible to gain an informed view from our judgments, since journalists could not judge the instances themselves. The contempt of court provision in the Act also protected the dignity of the Appeal Board and journalists were treading carefully. Truly a sad day for press freedom! When I took over as chairman in 1980, one of the first steps I took was to allow the press to attend all screenings with the Appeal Board. Some of them must have been disappointed: we were not watching porn, which simply went to the police for prosecution.

OF COURSE THERE WAS THE MULTITUDE of bans of possession on publications, which were sent to us for confirmation – mostly ANC, PAC and AZAPO-oriented* security material and pornography. In this category – and this provided some light relief at the time – we on one occasion received a large box of condoms described by the manufactures as "rough riders". At first glance they could easily have been mistaken for a box of tarantulas. We decided that the condoms did not fall within the definition of "objects" in terms of the Act. The Registrar sent the box back by registered train mail. Rumour had it that the box went astray in the wide open fields of the Karoo and never reached Cape Town where the Directorate of Publications was situated. Somewhere between De Aar and Matjiesfontein† a couple must have had some joy for quite a number of years …

A pump intended to address the affliction of impotence was also sent back for the same reason. Privately I was relieved about this decision, since I was wondering where we would find someone who would be prepared to put the gimmick to the test …

---

*   Organisations banned by the government.
†   Both well-known stops of the Blue Train to Cape Town from Johannesburg.

IN 1976 WE HEARD AN APPEAL AGAINST a ban on the distribution of hundreds of men's underpants. The underpants had a wide variety of phrases on them such as "my adorable nutcracker", "the drill that will never die", and "Custer's last stand" … Dr Klaas van Wyk de Vries, the theologian on the first Board, argued convincingly that underpants were a private matter and that they could not be indecent or obscene. The appellants were jubilant about the decision and conveyed to the clerk of the Board that he could keep the hundreds of *objets d'art*. The chairman, Judge Snyman, decided that he was not permitted to do so since it could be construed as a bribe. I have often wondered what one would do if one received five hundred underpants − would the stock last a lifetime and yes, would the inscriptions fade in the wash? What we did not foresee was that underpants were not really that private − the distributors placed them in full view of the public in shop window displays. A difficult nut to crack …

BY 1976 SOMEONE HAD ALSO PRODUCED wine goblets (definitely not in Venice or Prague, but probably in Braamfontein or Hong Kong), which portrayed scantily clad models on them. Certainly not the kind of goblet from which Alfredo would drink singing "Libiamo" in *La Traviata*. Apparently, as one sipped one's drink from a goblet the bikini would start disappearing until the model was entirely nude. A committee had banned the distribution, one of the reasons being that it would further alcoholic intake and could lead to lustful thoughts developing whilst one was becoming inebriated. We set aside the ban – the goblets which were sent to us to inspect (and possibly drink from?) did not seem to have the potential of successfully disrobing the models, in any case. The gimmick was simply not a good buy. I privately pondered at the time whether this would, in law, be regarded as a latent defect in the goblets or whether a court would not simply reject such an action on the basis that a buyer must be vigilant.

TO ILLUSTRATE CONSERVATIVE VIEWS at the time, the following incident is rather hilarious in retrospect, but it was pretty serious stuff at the time. Pieter-Dirk Uys is a renowned South African playwright and actor who pokes fun at almost all leaders, including Margaret Thatcher, British Prime Minister at the time, the then Minister of Sport and Recreation, Piet Koornhof and State President P.W. Botha. In 1979, Uys produced a play in which he mocked traditional Afrikaner values. A young attractive lady, dressed in full (Afrikaner traditional) Voortrekker dress (which consists of a long white frock and a bonnet and which are still worn at folk dancing), came onto the stage in full regalia. She sang a well-known song

which is often sung while doing folk dances (translated): "Afrikaners are joyous, and that can be believed! They love parties and then they do this." In the folk dance the partners would then bow and take some elegant steps. In the Uys show, the young lady (who went on to become quite a splendid South African movie actress) started doing a striptease on stage. I was acting as chairperson for that appeal and I recall one of my Afrikaans colleagues whispering into my ear during the striptease (while his eyes remained nailed to the spectacle): "God! No, this cannot be permitted. This strikes at the heart of Afrikaner values!" The audience was of course roaring with laughter.

The Appeal Board did not smile and ordered the scene to be cut on the grounds that it brought the Afrikaans section of the community's values into disrepute. I am embarrassed to admit that I wrote the judgment and omitted to file a minority judgment: I had found the scene absolutely hilarious. Hindsight is of course always a perfect sight (whatever the sight). In the same play Pieter-Dirk Uys had a character proclaiming that the censors were so strict that they had banned the names of two towns since they included obscene words: Kakamas and Nigel. Since this book is not meant to be sold subject to an age restriction, I will not explain why this was his view. This is clearly a matter for the informed reader to interpret and snigger at.

Personally I have no excuse for those pre-1980 times – I cannot deny that I was involved in the decisions made, and I must confess that I was pondering whether we were not far too strict. Being the youngest member at age 33, I was, however, probably more tolerant than my older colleagues, who were all over 50. I recall returning from Cape Town where I acted as chairman in an appeal from the Baxter Theatre where the co-opted members and I deemed it fit not to cut the word "shit" from a hilarious, mature play. On my return I was criticised by some of my colleagues for the indiscretion.

For the sake of interest a 1977 committee excised a scene from a film in which the Broederbond* was criticised as a deplorable or-

---

★   The Broederbond was a secret organisation for white males, which had a strong influence on the apartheid government. By 1994 the organisation was disbanded and the Afrikanerbond, its successor, is currently an organisation that solely furthers Afrikaner cultural interests. It is no longer secret.

ganisation. The committee reasoned that the Broederbond was a "section" of the population in terms of the Act. This was most certainly not the case and the Appeal Board reinstated the scene on appeal.

Another matter, which also drew laughs in the media, was the ban on the novel *The Odessa File*. In the book a bomb is rigged to a car engine and the car is blown up on ignition. The Committee felt that the description was likely to lead to a copycat by would-be saboteurs and banned the book as posing a danger to law and order. The media checked the efficacy of the bomb with experts, and published inserts ridiculing the bomb "which could not go off". Koos Pretorius, the Director of Publications, revoked the ban a week later.

To illustrate how conservative especially Afrikaans-speaking Christians were at the time, an Afrikaans newspaper carried comments against my being available as acting chairman to hear an urgent appeal against the ban of Spike Milligan's play, *The Bed Sitting Room,* on a Sunday evening. The criticism was exacerbated by the fact that God was impersonated in the closing scenes of the play. How could the Appeal Board be available to hear a matter of blasphemy on a Sunday, a church leader was quoted as having said. I went ahead and we saw the play on the Sunday evening. We upheld the appeal.

My endeavours in the eighties of freeing South Africa from despotic censorship laws – the subject of this book – was diametrically opposed to conservative doctrine. "How could an Afrikaner and Christian be so immoral as to allow nudity, profanity, crude language and sex in films?" And how could one ever justify the unbanning of the *Freedom Charter* in 1984 and *Cry Freedom!* in 1988?

Could this be a true Afrikaner, it was asked in the hallways. However, it was the very closeness to these draconian laws which had driven me towards freedom and fairness in the 1980s when I took over as chairman of the Appeal Board.

When Desmond Abernethy, the retired principal of Boys High in Pretoria, joined the Appeal Board in 1977, he brought a fresh breath of air with him. This was especially the case where religion and state security were involved. I remember his minority report on the ban of the film *Godspell* and his strong view that the *Inkatha* newspaper* did not promote revolution but merely stated the rights to which the disenfranchised majority was entitled. Desmond also became a staunch supporter of my liberating approach during the eighties.

The Nürnberg trial of Nazi leaders was almost replayed in Pretoria. A publication titled *Did Six Million Really Die?* was passed by a Publications Committee in 1977. The Jewish Board of Deputies wished to appeal, but the Act provided that only the Directorate could appeal where a publication had been passed. The Directorate of Publications appealed to the Appeal Board and Judge Snyman permitted the Jewish Board of Deputies to assist the Directorate's senior counsel to prepare and argue his case. I have a clear memory of Suzman, Queen's Counsel,† assisted by a number of juniors, walking into our court with stacks of documents. Albert Speer, the

---

*   The Inkatha Freedom Party newspaper.
†   Senior advocates were called either King's Counsel or Queen's Counsel when South Africa fell under the British sovereign. After independence in 1961, it was switched to Senior Counsel. However, senior advocates who had gained the status from the governor general before 1961, remained Queen's Counsel.

famous Minister of Armaments in Hitler's cabinet, filed a lengthy affidavit confirming that the publication was not true in claiming that the killing of Jews was a hoax. Thousands of pages from Jews who had been in concentration camps were also filed with us; all claiming that they knew first-hand that the gas chambers were operating in full force.

Senior counsel was briefed on both sides. After months of preparation we were just about to commence hearing this matter when there was a call from the Prime Minister, John Vorster. Judge Lammie Snyman asked me to listen in on the call: "Lammie! You would do South Africa a great favour if you cooled down this trial." Judge Snyman, who knew John Vorster well from their days at the Johannesburg Bar, was taken aback and we contemplated what to do. The matter was tabled before us and there was no way in which it could be "cooled down". Fortunately, we did not have to do anything. The next day the Directorate withdrew its appeal and the matter was removed from the Roll. This was an anti-climax for us. In hindsight we would never have brought the debate to a close! Of course, the evidence is overwhelming that Hitler had millions of Jews killed in gas chambers.

Other debates, as will be clear from the next chapter, would in any case take up our time in the next two years.

Trouble was in the air ...

THREE
Gert Garries of Magersfontein
1977–1980

TO PARAPHRASE DAPHNE DU MAURIER: last night I dreamt I was back at Magersfontein. Next to the road, watching the spectacle of cameramen and actors, stood Gert Garries. It was probably his conduct, hilariously described by Etienne Leroux in *Magersfontein, O Magersfontein!*, which led to the organised campaign from conservative quarters against this novel. Gert thought of sex with Rebecca Daisy and would not have heard of Du Maurier's grand novel, *Rebecca*, made into an Oscar winning Hitchcock thriller in 1941. When I awoke, my thoughts went back to a morning in Pretoria in 1977 …

On the tenth floor of the Civitas Building where the air-conditioned suite of the chairman of the Publications Appeal Board was situated, an important meeting was taking place. Seven men were seated around a conference table. The best satire ever written in Afrikaans was the subject of the meeting. "In heaven, chairman," thundered the impressive broadcaster's voice of Douglas Fuchs,*

★   Douglas Fuchs was involved in broadcasting during all his adult life and became the Director General of the SABC, retiring in 1976. He was known for his organisational skills and was called "god" at the SABC. He was closely associated with the doyen of South African poets and literary experts, N.P. van Wyk Louw. Douglas was renowned for his magnificent elocution and the capacity to formulate extremely well, both in English and in Afrikaans.

"great literature will never be written, since there is no sin in heaven!" Then the decisive voice of the chairman, Judge Snyman: "Yes, but here on earth a law applies and if God's Name is used in vain or a person uses crude language in a novel, even if it is part of a brilliant satire, the people and the law forbid it." "No!" cried Douglas, "great literature must always risk something!" "Not in law, Mr Fuchs, not in law!" the chairman's voice rang through his large chambers in Pretoria. And that sealed the ban on *Magersfontein, O Magersfontein!*

The satire had been on the shelves for several months and had in fact been found to be "not undesirable" by a publications committee. However, when orchestrated complaints from Afrikaans churches and other conservative Afrikaans organisations reached the Minister of Home Affairs he, after a discussion of the matter in the 1977 John Vorster cabinet, referred *Magersfontein* to the Publications Appeal Board. This was a dramatic moment since the author, Etienne Leroux, was an important author and in my mind the best satirist that South Africa had ever produced. But the satire contained crude language and instances where the Lord's Name was used in vain by some of the characters. One of the characters, Rosemary Marigold, would for example in the first part of the book often simply say "Jesus Christ".* She accompanied a foreign group which was planning to shoot a film of one of the historic battles between the forces of the Republics and the British forces during the Anglo-Boer War at Magersfontein, at the end of the nineteenth century.

---

*   Experts would explain that the taking of the Lord's Name was functional in that it described her agony at being of no value. Later in the book, when she assisted in rescuing people who were drowning, she demonstrated her role as someone who assisted other people and the profanities ceased.

A local spectator, Gert Garries, did not share these high ideals. While urinating, he thought of the magnificent sex he had had with Rebecca Daisy. His thoughts were described in crude, hilarious terms. On the carrier of his bicycle lay the body of his dead baby wrapped in linen; a body which he was on his way to bury ...

However, not everyone laughed. Excerpts from the satire (obviously not quoted in context) were circulated to churches and conservative Afrikaans organisations. Chris Barnard, a well-known author and scriptwriter later satirised the first formal complainant, a lady from the Free State, in Die Huisgenoot. He had hunted her down, had an interview with her and revealed that she had no knowledge of literature and had not even read the book. She, however, felt that as a Christian she was entitled to complain about what she had found offensive in the satire. She had heard that the novel included the taking in vain of the Lord's Name and crude language. Context was irrelevant. She felt such language could never be justified on literary grounds. Blasphemy remained blasphemy.

Before the hearing at the Appeal Board, there was a lively debate in the media as to whether the newly appointed Appeal Board would demonstrate more respect for literature than the previous Board and Supreme Court under the Act of 1963. The Court had in 1974 confirmed a ban by the Publications Board of Kennis van die Aand* by André P. Brink, who had become known as a "rebel" from the sixties and had been prepared to realistically describe sexuality and the plight of a coloured man in a sexual relationship with a white woman under the segregation laws of the apartheid regime, as explained earlier in this book.

★   *Looking on Darkness.*

Dr Piet Koornhof, the Minister of Sport and Recreation, who took a keen interest in literature and who was later on to become South Africa's ambassador to the United States, noticed the chairman of the Appeal Board and me, his deputy, having lunch in Pretoria (at the same restaurant with the Pritchard nudes described earlier!). He joined us for a few minutes and chatted about the pending matter of *Magersfontein, O Magersfontein!*, which had been referred to us by the Minister of Home Affairs, Dr Connie Mulder. In his well-known companionable style, he called upon us to not simply ban the book. He said he was sure that he was the only member of the Cabinet who had read the book and understood its satirical context. "Judge, I have been known to devise a boereplan* to solve and evade difficult situations within the South African apartheid context. Why don't you do the same with *Magersfontein, O Magersfontein!?*" he asked. The Judge answered that in law one did not make a "boereplan", as was the case in politics …

Douglas Fuchs, a former Director-General of the South African Broadcasting Corporation, and Alwyn Grové, Dean of the Arts Faculty at the University of Pretoria and the next chairman of the South African Academy for Science and Art, voted against the ban on the distribution of the satire by Etienne Leroux and filed a minority report. Ironically, they asked me privately to evaluate the minority judgment for them from a legal perspective, since I had voted with the chairman. Hardly two years later the Academy hit back with Alwyn Grové at its helm: Leroux was awarded the pres-

---

*   "Boereplan" means a solution which would not lead to a ban, but would
    also address some of the fears of the conservative sectors. Such a plan
    could, for example, have been that the book would only be available to
    adults on request.

tigious Hertzog prize for the banned *Magersfontein, O Magersfontein!* This was a crisis: if even the conservative Academy was against the publications control applied at the time, how would the new Publications Act (1974) ever survive?

The decision of the Appeal Board was taken on review to three judges of the Supreme Court. Johann Kriegler SC acted for the Board and Fanie Cilliers SC for the publishers Human & Rousseau. The argument took two days. Fanie Cilliers argued that the Board had incorrectly held that the Publications Act forbade it to consider the moral and religious tolerance of the likely reader which, in this case, was a sophisticated and intellectual reader. Johann Kriegler opened his argument by quoting one of the Ten Commandments: "Thou shalt not take the Name of the Lord in vain." He argued that this commandment was absolute and not subject to exceptions in terms of the Publications Act. Rykie van Reenen, a well-known columnist, opened her tongue-in-cheek comment in a Sunday Newspaper with the words: "Johann Kriegler becomes Preacher!" and referred to the words quoted above.

The Full Bench, consisting of Judge President Boshoff and Judges van der Walt and Myburgh, held that the Appeal Board had mistakenly decided that the Publications Act prohibited it to consider the views of likely readers of a publication in so far as morality was concerned. On the other hand, in so far as religion was concerned, the Appeal Board had correctly held that the likely readers were irrelevant. However, the likely readership could have an effect on the impact of the book in so far as religious feelings were concerned. The application for review was, accordingly, dismissed with costs. Later in the eighties, this judgment assisted me as successor to Judge Snyman, in introducing a new approach to literature. We could unban all the banned books of literary value, which included *Magersfontein, O Magersfontein!, Kennis van die Aand, Lady Chatterley's Lover* and even that great eighteenth-century lover, Fanny Hill in *Memoirs of a Woman of Pleasure* by John Cleland – probably the most prosecuted book in the history of prose. John Cleland wrote it while he was in debtors' prison …

DR ALWYN SCHLEBUSCH SUCCEEDED Dr Connie Mulder as Minister of Home Affairs in 1979. He inherited a crisis: the Board's approach to literature, notably *Magersfontein, O Magersfontein!*, had caused a rift between the Board and even conservative Afrikaans literary experts. To address this problem, Dr Schlebusch introduced into the legislation a Committee of Experts who would advise the Appeal Board on the literary or dramatic merits of a work. Shortly after this amendment to the Act, the chairman referred to it as "a sop to the writers" in a *Sunday Express* interview. This remark did not bode well for literature. The amendment also failed its first test. When *Donderdag of Woensdag** by John Miles came before the Board, the Committee of Experts advised that the profanities in the work should be read through a literary prism as an attack on despotism and not on religion – obviously the South African apartheid system. However, the chairman appointed Prof. Johan Heyns, the respected theologian, who advised that the book amounted to blasphemy. How could God be portrayed as menstruating and Jesus as saying "fuck"? And yet, the literary committee of thirteen explained that all these profanities were the profanities as seen from the per-

★   "Thursday or Wednesday" (1978).

spective of a sinner within a despotic (apartheid) structure. Such a person's god would do the things which the novel fictionally visualised: his god would be barren and his Jesus would use crude language. I must concede: on face value, the book was blasphemous. However, once one read the motivation of the Committee of Experts, one understood the reasoning from a literary perspective. But would the ordinary person read the book in this manner? Of course, the ordinary person did not read it. At the time it emerged that only some hundred persons had purchased the book and that the convoluted style would limit it to an extremely small, informed readership. But the limited likely readership was not regarded by the pre-1980 Appeal Board as having any special weight and it banned the book's distribution. Two years after I took over as chairman, we unbanned the book after I had a meeting with Prof. Heyns and Dr Rialette Wiehahn, the chairperson of the Committee of Experts. Prof. Heyns said that he respected the views of the experts and supported the lifting of the ban. I recently read the book again. How the book could ever have raised any issues as to undesirability in terms of the Publications Act, when read contextually, is surprising in this modern day and age.

In September 1979, Dr Alwyn Schlebusch took Judge Snyman and me for lunch to *Toulouse,* a top restaurant in Pretoria, and told us about his dilemma: he had as a matter of urgency pressed Parliament to accept the amendment to the Act and with enormous effort convinced fifteen literary experts to serve on the literary committee. *Now* they were threatening to resign since their view on *Donderdag of Woensdag* had been rejected by the Board and the opinion of an outside expert accepted – the expert not being a literary expert, but a professor in theology. Please, would the chairman in future deal more sensitively with the committee and not appoint a further expert to counter them. "No" said Judge Snyman, "I am a Judge and when I deem it to be in the interests of justice, I will appoint an expert from outside the committee." With that, Judge Snyman's future as chairman was placed at risk. However, I must laud him for his integrity – saying what he said despite the fact that he knew that his five-year term was almost at an end. On the other hand, Alwyn Schlebusch had opened up the possibility for the literary and dramatic input. This assisted me enormously as the next chairman in the eighties – to move for freedom for literary merit in books and dramatic merit in films.

FOUR

Magersfontein and other victories
1979–1984

I TOOK OVER AS ACTING CHAIRMAN on 3 October 1979: exactly twenty-two years after the Russians had placed Sputnik in space; eighteen years after *Lady Chatterley's Lover* had been held to be not obscene by a British jury; eighteen years after South Africa had become a Republic outside the Commonwealth; seventeen years after the first detention without trial legislation was enacted; five years before the legislative ban on sex between black and white was lifted; three years before Andries Treurnicht walked out on the National Party and founded the Conservative Party; and, yes, eleven years before Nelson Mandela was released from prison.

That afternoon we ruled that nudity was permissible in a 1974 Pirelli calendar.* This was a first. Unfortunately, it was not yet the grand issue with Sophia Loren, which was only to be published in 2007! Yet, it was a huge step away from the absolutism of the past.

Four months later, the Board unbanned *Magersfontein, O Magers-*

---

*   The Pirelli calendar is a trade calendar published by the Pirelli company's UK subsidiary dating back to 1964. The calendar is famous for its limited availability because it is not sold and is only given as a corporate gift to a restricted number of important Pirelli customers and celebrity VIPs. The Pirelli calendar is perhaps the world's only prestigious and exclusive "girly" calendar, featuring pictures generally considered glamour photography including artistic nudes.

fontein! It immediately hit the headlines. Freedom at last! The Committee of Experts and a Supreme Court judgment that held the likely reader to be relevant in deciding on indecency contributed towards saving the satire. In so far as religion was concerned we held that, read in context, the profanities did not amount to blasphemy. Although the taking in vain of the Lord's Name could be offensive to some readers, it was not legally offensive. The hilarious idiosyncrasies of Gert Garries on page 22 of the book was, at last, open to be read by all. Sam Maritz SC, who was instructed by the State Attorney to defend the ban on *Magersfontein, O Magersfontein!* in 1980, started laughing uncontrollably when he quoted one of the hilarious sentences from the book – and, in fact, his laughter turned into tears of laughter. He nevertheless put the case for the non-lifting of the 1977 ban well, but I do not think his heart was in it, given the laughter! The ban was lifted. Piet Streicher SC – later on to become a Judge of Appeal – acted for Human & Rousseau, the publisher.

A FEW DAYS AFTER THE UNBANNING of *Magersfontein, O Magersfontein!,* Minister Alwyn Schlebusch informed me that the State President wanted to appoint me as the new chairman. Would I fly down to Cape Town and meet him? He was considerate enough to tell me that it had nothing to do with the unbanning of *Magersfontein.* However, the unbanning must have been a relief to Dr Schlebusch. His concept of a literary committee had saved the day. All that he said to me at our first meeting was that he expected us to be "reasonable". I was 37 years old and concerned that I might not be acceptable to all the members of the Board, who were all over 50.

But Dr Schlebusch convinced me to take up the position and that the literary establishment would back me. As guaranteed by the Act, the Appeal Board would act independently from Government. I made an arrangement with the University of Pretoria according to which I would be seconded to the Board in a part-time capacity. As it turned out, I spent twenty hours a week on the Appeal Board work and in a sense it became what I regarded as my life's work; we dealt with 2000 appeals over the next decade. Each decision had to be motivated in a written judgment.

The heavy workload at the Appeal Board and the University meant that I often had to rush between the university and my chambers at the Appeal Board in the Pretoria city centre. By 1985 I had been appointed Deputy Dean of the Law Faculty. I recall working late into the nights dictating judgments and becoming increasingly aware of the daunting task that lay ahead of me – to free South Africa from the slavery of censorship. This ideal and its implementation changed my life dramatically. Inadvertently, I had become part of the struggle towards a new Democratic South Africa. Looking back today, I regard this as the greatest challenge of my career. To have achieved this ideal was the pinnacle of my life. When I chaired the drafting of the new Films and Publications Act after Democracy in 1994, I could ensure that South Africa would never again ban works of merit.

I was geared to institute a new approach to films and publications control – a control based on trust in adults to read and view what they chose to, and on age restrictions to protect children; a control which would also lead to the opportunity for the voice of the disenfranchised majority to be heard legitimately in publications, films and plays. That this was not official government policy was irrelevant to me. What counted was the freedom of expression and interpretation which, I thoroughly believed, should be attached to the Act. We simply had to move out of the Middle Ages in so far as literature, theatre and films were concerned. The reality and legitimacy of the voice of the disenfranchised majority could also no longer be ignored. To suppress it was politically and morally wrong. Once again this was not government policy. However, since I believed in the Appeal Board's guaranteed independence and was, and still am, a supporter of the functionalist legal school, the path which we would take was determined by a purposive interpretation of the Act of 1974.

I was able to convince the majority of my colleagues – often over a friendly lunch and good red wine (I had a good collection of Roodeberg 1972!) – to work towards a new goal of freedom. Forces which influenced me were my love of books, classical music, the theatre, films and editorial freedom. Splendid lawyers such as John Dugard, Gilbert Marcus, Lauren Jacobson, Mark Rosin, Nick Haysom, Edwin Cameron, Anton Mostert, Piet Streicher, Kathy Satchwell, Henning Viljoen, Johann van der Westhuizen, Louis van Wyk, Duard Kleyn and Christof Heyns all played a vital role in the formulation of principles when addressing us on behalf of publishers and film distributors. Of course, publishers, film distributors and theatre owners such as Jonathan Ball, David Philip, Jane Raphaely, Human & Rousseau, Penguin Books, Heinemann, Republican Publications, United International Pictures (Gerald Sobel), Ster-Kinekor (Bill Sharp and Robert Howie), The Baxter Theatre, The State Theatre and many more ensured that cases be put before the Appeal Board by these lawyers in more than 2000 appeals from 1980 to 1990. Once it emerged that a new freedom-oriented approach was being followed, the rate of appeals grew immensely.

SHORTLY AFTER MY APPOINTMENT as chairman in 1980, Dr Alwyn Schlebusch appointed the talented academic, Prof. Braam Coetzee, to the position of Director of Publications. His expertise lay in administration,* literature and theology. I found a splendid companion and close friend in Braam. We would sail the ship of dramatically increased freedom together for a decade: he as the head of the Directorate which appointed committees to decide on publications and films, and I as the chairperson of the appeal body which had the final say. After that I was privileged enough to have him with me on the 1994-1996 Task Group, which drafted the new Films and Publications Act within a new constitutional dispensation. Braam introduced classification for films early in 1990 and thereby laid the groundwork for what would be one of the cornerstones of the new Act.

WITH THE UNBANNING OF *Magersfontein, O Magersfontein!*, the first step was taken towards what would become our hallmark: freedom for adults to read literature and watch films of their choice and liberty to the disenfranchised majority to write, agitate for and read about a future unitary and democratic state governed by the majority. However, soft and hard pornography would remain forbidden. The pinnacle of freedom was not perceived to lie in porn. It lay elsewhere …

And this is where the slow road to decadence and loss of white political power commenced – at least, that is how moral funda-

---

*   He had been the Acting Rector of the University of Fort Hare, near Alice in the Eastern Cape.

mentalists and the vast majority of supporters of the government described the path which the newly chaired 1980 Board had decided to take. I received letters damning me as the antichrist. Others were not much kinder: how could I be a Christian and nevertheless vote to allow the taking in vain of the Lord's Name in books and films? When the open policy of the Board in regard to the disenfranchised majority became clear by 1988, my family's safety became a concern; a matter which I will discuss later. Braam Coetzee received similar threats. As the general administrator under the Act, he of course received many more letters and had to liaise with the public, government, churches, cultural organisations, writers' guilds and international colleagues. The Afrikaans churches were a major force in society and were seen by many as an arm of the national government, at least up to 1986.

Of course, the launch of the new freedom boat led to intense debate on the Board and in conservative circles. In 1983, Alwyn Grové, who had successfully testified against André P. Brink's *Kennis van die Aand* before the Supreme Court in 1974, despondently told me that the government would fire us when the Appeal Board set aside the 1974 Supreme Court ban on the book in 1983. Of course this was not legally possible, but the view expressed was representative of the rejection of Brink as a worthwhile author by a sector of the Afrikaans literary establishment. A view with which I did not agree and still do not agree. Brink has become a renowned, internationally acclaimed author and literary expert. In 1974 the Supreme Court had regarded the novel as offensive to the religious convictions of Christians, as described earlier in this book. At the core of the problem lay Joseph Malan's sexual relationship with a white woman (who happened to be British) and the parallel which was sought to be drawn between his suffering as a coloured person under the apartheid laws of segregation and the suffering of Jesus Christ. In 1983 the book's literary value, which had become relevant in the 1979 amendment to the Act, saved it from a ban. At last South Africans could also buy a book which many of them had only seen at bookshops abroad – often in translated form. The work had become famous internationally. Two other works of Brink, which reached the Appeal Board level, were also found to be not in contravention of the Act.

Interestingly enough, I received a call from the chairman of the Committee of Experts, Prof. Merwe Scholtz, who advised us on the literary merits of *Kennis van die Aand*. He was severely critical of the unbanning of the book. Yet, my reading of their report only discerned a critical note as to the literary merit. However, this was to my mind, not the only factor. The book, according to the view of the majority of the Appeal Board, had particular literary merit and was not, judged as a whole, offensive to the religious convictions of Christians. It was the first novel in Afrikaans that squarely opposed the apartheid policy – a necessary voice in troubled times. Dr Izak de Villiers, the respected Afrikaans poet and theologian, told me that Merwe Scholtz was not speaking for him and author Anna M. Louw, the two other members of the Committee of Experts. As members of the Committee of Experts, they were both for the approval of the novel.

I must add that by 1985 Prof. Grové had become a staunch supporter of the new approach to literature and when I left the Board in 1990, he was the one who held the farewell speech, kindly praising me for the courage to have introduced freedom for literature and drama in South Africa.

INTERESTINGLY ENOUGH, THE BAN on the Wilbur Smith novel, *When the Lion Feeds,* which had been confirmed by the Appellate Division of the Supreme Court in 1965 under the Act of 1963, was simply set aside in 1976 at first level under the new Act. No appeal was lodged to the Appeal Board by the Directorate of Publications. It was obvious that the famous minority judgment of Judge of Appeal Rumpff had, at last, won the day. The book was indeed innocuous from its inception. The 1965 ban by the majority of the Court illustrated the rigours of censorship in the sixties. To be honest the rigours of the majority judgment in the Appellate Division were to be repeated under the new Act in the next four years leading up to 1980.

After Judge Rumpff retired as Chief Justice, he was kind enough to regularly, as an expert, advise the Board on the interpretation of the Act. I asked him for an opinion as to the meaning of section 1 of the Act. The section provided that the constant endeavour of the South African populace to adhere to a Christian view of life should be acknowledged in the application of the Act. His interpretation was that the section referred to western values and was compatible with freedom of religion; it was also not a criterion in terms of the Act but, at most, a moral confession. When, later on, I was vehemently attacked in an article in a legal journal for ignoring section 1 of the Act, I could refer to the retired Chief Justice's opinion when the Minister, a successor of Dr Schlebusch, enquired from me how he should answer the query which he received from the State President's Office in view of the article. I never heard from the authors or the Minister again.

By 1984 there was also a 300-page document circulated to a large number of Afrikaans churches. The document contained the judgments in which the Appeal Board had set out its open policy as to the taking in vain of the Lord's Name in films. It condemned the Board for this policy, which was regarded as being in conflict with the Word of God. It led to agitated letters to the Minister, which were answered by Braam Coetzee, the Director of Publications. Personally, as the leader elder in my church, I found this attack most disconcerting. However, officially we ignored these attacks and sped forth on our road to freedom of choice for adults.

IN THE EIGHTIES I CONVINCED THE Appeal Board that the test for harmfulness had to be a *real* test. Only if material was in fact likely to promote what was generally regarded as morally evil, could one apply the harmfulness test. The result was that we almost never resorted to the test anymore. What was the content of public morality in any case? Section 1 of the Act of 1974, in conflict with the common law principle of freedom of religion, determined this morality to be that of Christians.* This could simply not be true and we regarded it as a moral confession supporting western values – as advised by Judge Rumpff. Therefore, when *The Rocky Horror Picture Show* came before us on review in the eighties, we passed it with an age restriction and without cuts. It was simply a cult movie and a send-up on thrillers.

The "lab" was, at last, open to inspection.

---

* Although reference was made to section 1 during the first five years, we realised that the section did not comply with the principles of freedom of religion and was, in any case, too vague to apply.

BUT THE WORK OF THE NEWLY CHAIRED Board was not without mistakes. Indeed "freedom is a long walk" as wisely stated by Nelson Mandela in the last paragraph of his *Long Walk to Freedom*. The 1980 Board erred when it made a cut in a 1983 Robert Kirby play, *It's a Boy!* In this comedy, a young white girl takes her boyfriend home – a black man. At the time sexual relationships (which included "sexual kissing") between whites and blacks were still prohibited by the Sexual Offences Act. When the black boyfriend arrived, he kissed the girl in the presence of her conservative father, who nearly had what he called a "conorary". The majority of the Board ordered that the kiss be cut. It was of interest that the two theologians on the panel were against the cut and joined me in the minority: they argued that they could not support the cut since the kiss was not immoral. How right they were. On the lighter side, the kiss was removed in accordance with the order of the Board, but the playwright got around this in an unusual way. The very next night, when the kiss was about to take place, one of the father's white friends stepped in and kissed the white girl "on behalf" of the black man. He said he did not want anyone breaking the law. Kirby said this insertion raised many extra laughs.

Later in 1983 the Board took a clear stand on the Sexual Offences Act, stating that to cut scenes from a film based on a Nadine Gordimer* short story where a young white farmer had sex with a black girl, would amount to stifling the debate on the relevant section of the Act. Films had to be part and parcel of the debate which was current at the time and must have contributed to the extremely hurtful section 16 being repealed.

---

*   In the nineties she was awarded the Nobel Prize for Literature.

In a satirical revue by Robert Kirby, *Academy Rewards*, he satirised several apartheid-inspired traditions: amongst others mixed marriages. In one of the scenes, the minister who consecrated the marriage between a black man and a white woman asked the groom whether he took this "madam" to be his lawfully wedded wife, pronounced the married couple as "boy and wife" and instructed the groom to leave the church through the servants' entrance!

Bishop Desmond Tutu, the later Nobel Peace Prize laureate, was called by Kirby to testify on his behalf. The Bishop duly appeared before the Appeal Board and testified that it would be wrong to "cleanse" the play of derogatory language and thereby, as it were, ignore the shocking reality that this was the way in which many whites spoke to blacks. He said that, in fact, the mixed marriage sketch amounted to a profound theological statement, arguing that the Bible disavows marriage between people of different faiths but not people of different colour. Bishop Tutu also gave his view about another sketch in which an imaginary professor introduced a so-called "Bonsai Bantu", a scientifically miniaturised black person, speaking of the advantages of reducing all black people to a manageable size ... The Bishop testified that ideologically this was exactly what the apartheid government was attempting to do and that the sketch was part and parcel of political satire, which was necessary within that oppressive state.

The Board accepted the Bishop's arguments and the banning of both sketches was lifted. In a sense, the bonsai sketch was so true and, of course, satirised the inhuman ideas of the apartheid regime. In the early nineties I remember chatting with the Archbishop at an airport about his evidence at the hearing. I was impressed by his good humour when I referred him to his significant testimony, which I have often quoted in later years – including judgments of the Broadcasting Complaints Commission. It is to the credit of Prof. Fanie van Jaarsveld, whom I co-opted and who was a professor at the Law Faculty at the University of Pretoria, that he convinced me at the hearing to admit the evidence of the Archbishop.

FIVE

The scope of nudity in the eighties
1980–1990

WHEN I TOOK OVER AS CHAIRMAN of the Appeal Board in 1980 we followed a policy according to which "lust" would no longer be the test. It was too vague and subjective a test. What we did do was simply to say that nudity depicting female nipples, the pubic area and genitals would not be permitted in popular magazines. All kinds of silly coverings – tiny flowers, minute nipple caps and even added "censor" stars were used to cover female nipples.

Scope's owner, Republican Publications, an affiliate of Perskor, which was known to be a rather conservative publisher, found itself between Scylla and Charybdis: we were no longer banning *Scope* and it would seem to have been *Scope* policy (probably under orders from its conservative owner, Perskor) not to move into nudity itself and test the waters.

There was a possibility of a review to the Supreme Court, but since three judges had to sit in such a case, it would not seem to have been that easy to follow that route. Given the heavy workload of judges it was in any case probably difficult to urgently constitute a court of three judges on a Friday afternoon. And of course at the time, the ambit of review was more limited than is currently the case. Our view was that once nudity was allowed in popular magazines, this would lead to soft pornography being available freely.

However, art magazines and books did not have this problem.

In lighter vein, Schalk van der Merwe, the CEO of Republican Publications, said to me in jest over lunch that we would do their sales a favour if we were to ban *Scope* again. It was indeed true: the bans were often counterproductive and caused sales to soar. The head of the State Library in Pretoria told me that when it became known that *Magersfontein, O Magersfontein!* could be banned, there was a large number of enquiries about the book – often clearly from people who had no interest in the literary qualities of the book but rather in what was said by Gert Garries on page 22. Or possibly they thought that there would be some great sex scenes in *Magersfontein*, which there of course were not.

NUDITY ON STAGE – AND I AM NOT even mentioning sex – was initially taboo. I remember how a short glimpse of a female breast was permitted early in the 1980s. By 1988 we were still quite strict: an adult man in a comedy performed in the State Theatre Pretoria, appeared in the nude for what must have been twenty seconds. I think he might have "jumped" (or was it "sprung"!) from what was described as an artificial womb! The Appeal Board found the scene to have been indecent. The scene had no functional value and seemed to have been introduced merely for the sake of nudity. The next night the producer simply clad the actor in a huge white nappy … South Africa was clearly still in its infant stage in so far as nudity on stage was concerned. By that time nudity in age-restricted films was permitted without much browbeating.

However, in 1988 the Appeal Board permitted the Warehouse at the Market Theatre to feature nude breasts in a play called *Sunrise*

City. The following passage from the judgment illustrates the re-spect which had developed for dramatic merit:

> Miss Jacobson most ably argued that by its very nature experimental
> theatre re-examines the old, explores the new and pushes at tradi-
> tional theatrical boundaries in order to explore novel, exciting and,
> most importantly, relevant ways of perceiving current situations. She
> also quite rightly argued that the Committee seems to be alone in the
> view that the performance is "mediocre, without any artistic or dra-
> matic merit.

After that the stage was set for nudity. In a 1985 play at the Baxter, *Weed Killers,* we had no problem in finding that a scene where prisoners had to place their private parts on a bar for inspection, was not indecent. The scene was functionally and dramatically essential.

I understand that strip shows in some entertainment spots are quite common nowadays. Currently, public entertainment is dealt with in terms of indecency and liquor laws, since live public entertainment was not included by Parliament in the Films and Publications Act of 1996. This was done on the advice of the Ministerial Task Group. Consultation with several producers indicated that theatre productions should not be regulated as regards content. If age restrictions were necessary, they would impose these restrictions themselves and in other instances common law and legislative enactments would take care of possible abuse.* This has proved to be a success and is proof that self-control can work well; and this result is obviously a feather in the cap of the Task Group.

---

* Even under the Act of 1974 plays were not subjected to pre-control. The Directorate of Publications had a discretion as to whether it would react to complaints. During the fifteen years that I was involved with the Appeal Board, the Board probably did not attend more than thirty plays, including two or three strip shows.

SIX

A peek into porn in the nineties
1991-1998

IN AN EARLIER CHAPTER I SAID THAT our ideal was not to move into porn in the eighties. There were much more important issues to address. For the porn trade it was a time of drought. But with the first signs of a new Constitution that would guarantee freedom of expression, the "rains came". It was, most certainly, not the rains which flooded India in Louis Bromfield's great 1937 novel (made into an academy award-winning film – for best special effects – with Tyrone Power in 1939 and Richard Burton and Lana Turner in 1955), but the downpour and floods were essentially the same! When South African versions of the magazines *Penthouse, Hustler* and *Playboy* hit the stands early in the nineties, and it was clear that a new Constitution would guarantee freedom of expression, the market was flooded with soft porn within three years. *Scope*, which was clearly not prepared to go as far as *Penthouse* and *Hustler* (and its Afrikaans version, *Loslyf*), decided to close shop by 1996. *Playboy*, with its stylised nudity, was not wild enough for the seemingly famished South African market. It was simply not selling well and stopped its local issue after only a year. It was as if the flood gates had opened for real soft porn after a great drought. I do not think it is apocryphal that many South Africans in the pre-1990s on their visits abroad, would make *Playboy, Playgirl* or *Penthouse* their first buy.

The technique employed by *Penthouse* in 1991, after years of bans on nudity in popular magazines, was to publish one rather small photograph of a model with one nude breast in the sun, as it were, and the other in the shade. By that time I had already left the Appeal Board and was watching from the wings what was happening. Formidable as the approach was at the time, a publications committee banned the issue because of the solitary nude breast. An appeal was lodged to the Appeal Board by *Penthouse*. The ban was lifted within a few days by the Appeal Board and from there the nudes were increased every month until the stage was reached where sex photographs were published by 1993. The sales of *Hustler* were soaring while *Penthouse,* which had a more conservative policy, was experiencing problems with its sales which, at one stage, had gone up to over 100 000 copies per month. Ralph Boffard, *Penthouse's* local chief executive was on record that he would not permit the photographs in *Penthouse* to move into the standard of what he referred to as "gutter sex".

DURING THAT TIME I MET KATHY KEETON in New York, an ex–South African stage entertainer, who was running Penthouse International with her husband. Their splendid collection of impressionist art and the replica of an antique Roman bath downstairs in their New York Central Park villa fascinated me. It did not seem as if anyone ever bathed in it, in spite of the steam which surrounded the bath. For a moment I thought I saw what would seem to have been Bathsheba by Rembrandt with King David's letter in her hand sitting at the bath with King David peering at her from his castle. A copy of it in *Scope* might have been banned back in 1974!

Kathy Keeton shared the view of Ralph Boffard as to the limits which should apply. Of course, compared to earlier editions, *Penthouse* was still very explicit. The ban on nudes was part of a not so distant South African past.

There was an unexpected reaction from some segments of the public. Cafés stocking *Penthouse* et cetera were listed and informed by pressure groups that they would no longer be supported by regular customers. The *Penthouse* billboard designed to be put up at airports was not permitted by the Airport Authority and Braam Coetzee, the Director of Publications, was flooded with letters from shocked members of the public, churches and cultural organisations.

However, the police were still raiding porn shops in terms of the Indecent or Obscene Photographic Matter Act of 1967. Two convicted distributors took the matter to the Constitutional Court, which declared the criteria in that Act to be incompatible with constitutional values in 1996.[*] The Act had prohibited the possession of indecent photographs. Within the context of that Act, indecency, in practice, included soft porn. The Constitutional Court held the term "indecency" to be wider in ambit than the Constitution permitted and that it could also lead to the ban on possession of renowned works of art. However, the Court cautioned that its decision did not mean that the possession of some forms of pornography, notably child pornography, could not be validly prohibited. In 2003 the Court, in the *De Reuck*[†] case, in fact confirmed the

---

[*]   *Case and Another v Minister of Safety and Security and Others; Curtis v Minister of Safety and Security and Others* 1996(3) SA 617(CC).

[†]   2004(1) SA 406(CC).

constitutionality of such a prohibition, after substantially limiting the effect of section 27 of the Films and Publications Act of 1996 (as amended in 1999). Hereby the Court followed the trend in several other countries: the USA, Germany, Canada, Ireland, the United Kingdom, Belgium and the Netherlands, to name but a few. I shall again refer to the issue of the protection of art in Chapter 13.

An attempt by Joe Theron, publisher of *Hustler* (South Africa), to have the Publications Act of 1974 declared unconstitutional in 1997 by way of a declaratory order, failed. Under the circumstances, the Constitutional Court* held that since it had a discretion whether to issue a declaratory order or not, it did not deem it appropriate to issue such an order. Justice Didcott also stated that a new Films and Publications Act was about to become operative and that it would, in all probability, be brought before the Court for scrutiny sooner or later.

As matters turned out, the new Act only became operational by mid-1998: an Act which I was privileged to draft as chairman of a Task Group appointed by the Minister of Home Affairs, Dr Buthelezi, in 1994. No provision of the Act, as originally passed, has ever been challenged in the Constitutional Court. The 1999 amended section 27 (child pornography) was challenged in 2003 for vagueness and having been too widely drafted in the *De Reuck* matter. The Constitutional Court narrowed down the provision substantially and dismissed the challenge. In its "narrow" version the section was almost similar to the section which we drafted in 1994. The Court even read in an exemption as regards child pornogra-

---

*   *JT Publishing (Pty) Ltd and Another v Minister of Safety and Security and Others* 1997(3) SA 514(CC).

phy depicted in art. The Task Group had proposed such an exemption in the case of child pornography, but it was not accepted by Parliament. Ironically, it was brought back by way of interpretation by the Constitutional Court. This judgment illustrates that whatever Parliament might intend, it is always bound by the Constitution.

Some provisions in the 2004 and 2009 amendments to the Act are so drastic that they remind one of pre-1980 times. A section which forbids citizens and permanent residents to do anything in a foreign country which the Act forbids them to do in South Africa, is absurd. Does this, for example, mean that if a citizen distributes XX material in a country where it is not forbidden, he or she could be prosecuted here? Or, to make it even more difficult, if a South African citizen possesses child pornography for purposes of research in the USA, Canada, the UK, Ireland or Germany, where it is legal to do so, could he or she be prosecuted here for having done so? The answer is yes, since even such possession is not legal here. The mere fact that a Director of Public Prosecutions must authorise such a prosecution does not validate the provision.

SEVEN

The masses shout "Decadence"!
1980-1990

AFTER THAT GLIMPSE INTO THE FUTURE, I wish to take you back into the past! The unbanning by the newly chaired 1980 Board of *Lady Chatterley's Lover, Memoirs of a Woman of Pleasure, Kennis van die Aand, Donderdag of Woensdag, Portnoy's Complaint* and other works of merit followed soon after the unbanning of *Magersfontein, O Magersfontein!* in 1980. Literary merit* had, at last, won the day. More popular novels, of lesser merit, were also not banned. At times we used the 18-years-of-age restriction on sales to counter criticism that teenagers would be buying the books. I had gained the full cooperation of the Overseas Publishers Association over lunch for this project – if we could pass more books, they were happy to introduce age restrictions on sales. John Allen had arranged the meeting. *The Women's Room* by Marilyn French was the first book approved with an age restriction on its sales.

It was quite an event when we unbanned *Lady Chatterley's Lover* in 1981. The Board was not unanimous. Prof. Grové felt that the novel was not genuine in its description of the love affair of Lady Chatterley and the gamekeeper. The gamekeeper was representative of the working class which would ultimately overcome the

---

*   In the case of *Memoirs of a Woman of Pleasure*, it was probably historical literary interest.

rich classes by dominating them sexually. Douglas Fuchs, Nic Sabbagha, Desmond Abernethy, Kotie de Jager, Piet van der Merwe and I felt that it was high time that the book should be available in South Africa: the honesty and intimacy in the sexual relationship justified the use of the word "fuck" in its primary sense. The Committee of Experts* was, not surprisingly, unanimous in its advice that the novel had particular literary merit. This accorded with the expert advice in the American and British trials.

At the hearing of the matter our court room was packed with journalists. Close to the end of the trial, colleague Douglas Fuchs quoted extensively from the last pages in the book which, of course, include frequent use of the word "fuck" in its primary sense. He did this in a Shakespearean actor's style and from memory. The Bard would have been proud of him. One of the more senior, rather bulky, journalists in the public gallery, was so impressed (he had obviously heard Fuchs on the radio in the sixties when, according to Fuchs, he used to "canonise" recently deceased political leaders by broadcasting – in his own voice – a résumé of their lives in the service of the "people", with a background of Mozart's 21st piano concerto ...) that tears ran from his eyes; or was it mere perspiration in the stuffy court room? I will never know. In any case, I don't know whether he had ever heard the "word" in its primary sense in a formal setting. I certainly had not.

---

* The Commmitee of Experts had a number of females on it, in contrast to the Appeal Board, which had only one female, Anna Neethling-Pohl, who had decided to retire in November 1980. Prof. Réna Pretorius, a literary expert, was the other female member as from 1981. Danie du Toit, a film and art expert, joined the Committee of Experts as chairman. His leadership contributed to the unbanning of numerous films. Dr Rialette Wiehahn also played a prominent role as chairman.

To illustrate the serious debates and different opinions which we, at times, had at the post-1980 Appeal Board, I recall how some members expressed shock at sex references and sex scenes when we considered Philip Roth's hilarious satire, *Portnoy's Complaint* and John Updike's *Rabbit is Rich*. On both occasions Douglas Fuchs would, as it were, look for trouble, by quoting sex scenes or references from the two books out of context. To repeat the references here would also be out of context. Portnoy's obsession with masturbation and his rejection of traditional Jewish values throughout the book is sufficient to summarise the complaints from some members of the public against the "two million bestseller". The book is of course a satire and we ultimately released it unanimously. I recently read it again and enjoyed it thoroughly. One wonders what inspired any person in his right mind to have thought that this book was indecent.

In so far as *Rabbit* was concerned, the middle-aged motorcar salesman did not limit his sexual escapades in a "swinging" episode to what may be called conventional sex. Rabbit was, however, not that inventive himself; his seemingly conservative, rather unattractive partner taught him a few things that night. For Rabbit a shower would never be the same again.

In spite of its sensitive theme of adult-teenage love, Vladimir Nabokov's *Lolita* was approved without a stir and given an age restriction. Literary merit had clearly been accepted as a dominant factor. A translated version of the *Kama Sutra* also made the cut after a debate or two about the accompanying drawings.

A PROBLEM WITH THE ACT OF 1974 was that on a literal reading of section 47(2) it was obligatory to ban the distribution of a book when it "or any part of it" was indecent or obscene or offensive to public morals. The isolated-passage approach to censorship was anathema to literary experts and legal scholars such as Prof. Ellison Kahn, who published an article in the SA Law Journal on the ban on *When the Lion Feeds.* Chief Justice Steyn was criticised for apparently having applied this approach in banning the distribution of the novel. However, his successor, Chief Justice Ogilvie Thompson, rejected this isolated-passage approach and my directions to the Appeal Board in the eighties were that context was crucial in judging a work. When in 1994 we drafted the new Films and Publications Act of 1996, we ensured that the words "judged in context" ran through the Act as a golden thread: my past experiences of quotes out of context in order to condemn a novel, ensured that context be repeated everywhere. After Parliament attempted to exclude context in a 1999 amendment of section 27 on "child pornography", the Constitutional Court in 2003 rejected any approach according to which context would not be relevant. The 1994 Task Group was vindicated by this judgment: context would be relevant everywhere, even in the case of alleged child pornography.

THE NEXT ADVENTURE FOR THE 1980 BOARD lay in films and theatre. The pre-1980 approach was that any word that would not be acceptable in mixed company would be cut. As already mentioned, the word "fuck" was cut from the mafia-like *Scarface* in 180 spots; even the word "whore" was cut from the end credits of the film.

Words such as "shit" and all derivatives from "fuck" did not stand a chance. I need not mention the other, more crude, words. All nudity and even a scene where sex was implied under a blanket were cut. Inexplicit sex, which could be seen by viewers, was taboo, even for adult viewers. Even limited likely viewers and age restrictions did not save any material. However, on the so-called black market, pornography was freely available. Of course, possession of any pornography (even in *Playboy*, where the nudes, most certainly, did not fall in this category) was an offence.

To illustrate the dramatic difference between pre-1980 times and what was permitted post-1980 in theatre, the following incident should provide a light moment. In 1977 the chairman sent me to attend an Afrikaans Pieter-Dirk Uys play at the Market Theatre in Johannesburg. The play was called *Die Van Aardes van Grootoor*. The play poked fun at typical traditional Afrikaans values and apartheid leaders such as Dr Malan and Dr Verwoerd. A middle-aged lady was seen sitting cat-napping in a rocker. She wore a black Voortrekker dress and a bonnet. She said nothing but was constantly passing, what was heard to be, noisy winds. We cut the noises and held that this portrayal was ridiculing the Afrikaner woman as a section of the population. Koos de la Rey, the advocate who acted for the Market Theatre, phoned me the next day and asked whether they could leave in three of the twenty noises. The Board reconsidered the matter, but was adamant: "A fart is a fart", exclaimed Douglas Fuchs, whether it was the result of one or twenty!

It is difficult to keep a straight face when writing this now. But those were truly stifling times. I recall the distrust my colleague General Gideon Joubert displayed when he sat next to me in the audience at a side theatre of the Market, watching the *Van Aardes*.

He had a pistol with him. If one bears in mind that as a young officer, years before he became Commissioner of Police, he patrolled the area around the Market for smugglers and pickpockets, I have some understanding of his diligence. All that was now left at the Market were the winds of change.

In 1980 Athol Fugard's *The Island* was approved by us at the Baxter in spite of crude language throughout the play. The play dealt with the plight of political prisoners on an island, obviously Robben Island near Cape Town. There were complaints from the public about the language. However, the language fit the situation and characters so well that cuts were unthinkable. It was decided that an age restriction would take care of children and even act as a warning for more sensitive adult viewers. The newly chaired Board was on its way towards accepting realism and the past was disappearing at a quick pace!

The often hard-hitting dialogue in the Heiner Müller satire, *Quartett*, was also passed without cuts in 1981. This was quite an achievement, since even the Pope was denigrated in the satire and crude and profane language was used freely. I remember how Douglas Fuchs broke the silence as we all sat in my hotel room afterwards by suddenly saying: "That was bizarre!" It was indeed bizarre, bearing in mind the raw sexuality which permeated the play in dialogue and movement between the man and the woman: the woman at one stage even attaching a male genital prosthesis to herself and then cutting it off in reaction to male dominance. We passed the play without cuts …

SHORTLY AFTER I BECAME CHAIRMAN in 1980, the movie *Lady Chatterley's Lover* came before us on appeal. Sylvia Kristel – known for her (at the time) provocative scenes in the *Emmanuelle* series of the early seventies, which was then regarded as soft pornography – acted the role of Lady Chatterley. A Lady Chatterley who was, by implication, shown to masturbate in one scene and stare longingly at a gamekeeper through the window of the castle where she and her disabled husband lived. The film, no doubt, did not live up to the merits of the D.H. Lawrence novel. Yet, it was beautifully shot with stunning scenes of the misty English landscape. Yes, and of course, there was a scene where the full frontal nude gamekeeper could be seen bathing himself and the lady catching a longing glimpse at him and, ultimately, the love scenes and the use of the word "fuck" in its primary sense. Bill Sharp, the brilliant radio personality, argued the case for Ster-Kinekor Films, in whose employ he was. He won the case and the first nudity on screen and the first use of the word "fuck" in its primary sense had made its way onto South African screens. I received a signed photograph through the post from Sylvia Kristel with the words: "To Kobus, thanks for passing my movie." I, however, never met her, as it were, in the flesh.

Another movie which drew much interest was *Mata Hari,* based on the sexual adventures and semi-nude dances of the World War I double-agent known as Mata Hari (1876-1917).* At the time the

---

* Her real name was Gertrude Margarete Zelle. She lived in Java with her husband, a Dutch colonial officer. In 1901 she deserted him for Europe where she called herself Mata Hari. She sold her services on the basis that she had been a former temple dancer of Javanese origin. She worked for both the German and French intelligence services. The French executed her as a spy. See Clark (ed) *Illustrated Biographical Dictionary* (1978).

veil on nude female breasts had hardly begun to be lifted and there was quite a stir when we decided to pass the film with an age restriction of 18. The majority report from the Committee of Experts, chaired by Danie du Toit, was that the nudity was in character and not obscene. The cliché "pornography is in the eye of the beholder" was at the core of the Committee's discussion, I understand.

This brings to mind the words of Potter Stewart of the US Supreme Court:* "I shall not today attempt further to define (obscenity) … and perhaps I could never succeed in intelligibly doing so. But I know it when I see it." Locally, Justice Albie Sachs, a South African Constitutional Court Judge, said in 1996:

> Mr Justice Potter Stewart might have known obscenity when he saw it, but with respect, I do not, nor would I lay claim to any intuitive and immediate recognition of what is indecent. I am sure that the great majority of South African judicial officers, not to speak of police and prosecuting authorities, or of the general public, are in the same position. Far from the definition in the Act helping us, it amplifies the confusion by introducing such vague concepts as manifesting licentiousness and lust; discriminating against same-sex activities; and permitting the penalisation of possession of perhaps half the videos on sale in the most respectable of shops, and possibly three-quarters of coffee-table art books, let alone many tastefully illustrated copies of the Bible or Shakespeare.†

---

* See *Jacobellis v Ohio* 378 US 184 at 197.

† See *Case and Another v Minister of Security* 1996(3) SA 617(CC).

The Judge was commenting on the Indecent or Obscene Photographic Matter Act, in which the terms indecent or obscene were the criteria. They were held to be too vague to be constitutionally compatible and the Act consequently lost its efficacy. The new 1996 Films and Publications Act does not include such vague terms and the Task Group which advised Parliament, had already rejected these terms as too vague in 1994.

A STRANGE FEATURE OF CONSERVATIVE AFRIKAANS society would seem to have been that if nudity or sex were present in an English film or book, greater tolerance would be shown. Kas van den Berg, a well-known South African columnist and author once remarked in one of his columns that a man could, judged by the strict standards of censorship in the seventies and before that, take a woman to bed in English but not in Afrikaans. In 1985 a local producer included a rather explicit sex scene in a film called *Nag van Vrees* (night of terror). On appeal we reinstated the scene but added an age restriction of 2-18, which the producer agreed to. A cartoon in the daily *Beeld* showed two conservatively dressed Afrikaans-speaking men leaving a cinema after having seen the film. One observed that sex in Afrikaans does not differ from sex in English! A friend, who had invested in the film at the time, recently told me that the high age restriction did not result in an increase in the number of viewers. In fact, it almost destroyed the venture from a financial perspective. The film was released during the school holidays in 1985 and the fathers rather sat on the beach gazing at the very real scenes of skimpy bikinis while their teenage sons and daughters were shown away from the cinemas when attempting to gain access (according to another cartoon) under the guise of lipstick, stockings, fake moustaches and beards, trousers and jackets.

I remember how in 1957, as a 14-year-old boy, I slipped into an age-restricted (18) film and waited in vain for Brigitte Bardot to do something provocative. I cannot remember whether it was *And God Created Woman* (1956) or *That Crazy Kid* (1955). The censors had obviously seen the allegedly provocative scene before me and cut it! Or possibly the rumoured scene was never there. Even South African adults were not permitted to have a closer look at the famous sex goddess in a monokini. Americans would not even permit the sight of a female midriff in their own films, but when it was French, well, then different norms applied! But those were crazy times. So even if Jane Russell's midriff was regarded as risqué in *The French Line* (1953), the US cinemas could get away with some nudity by advertising a film as "French". Speaking of Brigitte Bardot, it has been said that she had done more at the time for the French balance of payments than the entire French vehicle industry. Of course, Brigitte Bardot was also a splendid actress. She demonstrated this in *Love on a Pillow* (1962).

LAST TANGO IN PARIS, ONE OF THE FIRST FILMS which included explicit sex scenes almost from the word go, has had its own dramatic censorship history. By 1987 we had at least approved the film, but with cuts and a 2-21 age restriction. United International Pictures (UIP) stated that they would not place this work of art on the South African circuit if it still had cuts. So, two years later they resubmitted the film and after consideration, one cut was left. Two years later, after I had left already, the Board reinstated the scene which was previously cut. One has to admire UIP's Gerald Sobel for his perseverance. I agree, one could not screen the film with cuts. D.H. Lawrence correctly argued that to cut a work of art would be comparable to attempts to cut parts of one's nose away. But that is the path of censorship: it often takes time to gain perspective ... or tolerance.

I recall how I watched *Last Tango in Paris* on the M-Net channel in 1995 and wondered what all the fuss had been about. No complaints were ever received by the Broadcasting Complaints Commission. By the end of the eighties I had almost reached one of my objectives: to permit adults to view films of quality (and even of lesser quality) without cuts (*Last Tango in Paris* was an exception, where I could simply not convince my colleagues). As to nudity I believe that *The Venus Trap, The Unbearable Lightness of Being, Dangerous Liaisons* and the Dutch film *The Fourth Man* probably illustrated this policy the best. However, we were using all the legal mechanisms at our disposal: some films were limited to art theatres while others were subjected to a 2-21 age restriction. Of course, the 2-21 restriction was intended to be more of a warning to sensitive viewers than a realistic restriction. In fact, by 1989 I had succeeded in reducing it to 2-19. We were not yet permitted by law to use classification symbols – that was officially only introduced in the nineties.

The best example was the first film allowed in 1984 under the art theatre condition, Kubrick's *A Clockwork Orange,* with its shocking juvenile delinquency and rape scenes. I have memories (nightmares?) of the accompanying song of the raping and destroying thugs: "Just singing in the rain!" And then, the sad image of the thug who had been released from prison after having been subjected to the in-thing of the early seventies: conditioning. Even sadder was his hate of Beethoven's 9th symphony after the treatment. Earlier in the film he was shown to love the 9th symphony. In fact, this was probably his only love. The treatment, which subjected him to continuous movie scenes of terrible violence, had inadvertently included the 9th as background music. So, the conditioning towards a hate for violence, had this extraordinary Beethoven fan as a victim. Of course, the film (and the book) was aimed at countering conditioning as a solution to the violent crime rate.

In 2010 the SABC broadcast the film after 21:45 with an 18 age restriction and full classification advice. Complaints were received at the Broadcasting Complaints Commission. I watched the film again and was, once again, struck by the terrible opening scenes, which were of course very relevant to the film. The Commission held that the broadcast, with full classification, did not transgress the Broadcasting Code.

Another Kubrick film, *Full Metal Jacket*, aimed against the violence in the Vietnam War, was tabled before the Board in 1989. The profane and crude language of the tough sergeant major in his training of marines led to a heated discussion as to whether an age restriction of 19 would be sufficient. There was also a suicide scene which was quite explicit. We had been employing the 21 age restriction mainly as a warning and knew that it was ridiculous to keep persons who had been to the army and other young people who were obviously in daily contact with crude language, away from the film. In a minority judgment I put forward the 19 age restriction and after that, it substituted the 21 age restriction. When we drafted the new Films and Publications Act in 1994, we explicitly excluded any age restriction higher than 18.

BEFORE I CONCLUDE THIS CHAPTER, the so-called "G-spot" deserves mention. *Sarie,* an Afrikaans woman's magazine from Nasionale Pers quarters, published an article on the "newly" discovered G-spot in 1983. Conservative female Afrikaans organisations were up in arms about the sexually intimate article: this would promote experimentation by teenagers, the banners and letters read. I sought the advice of five women and their opinion was that the article was not harmful and, indeed, promoted knowledge of sexuality. The Board accepted their advice and I lost a few female friends. On the other hand, another friend told me that her 70-year-old mother was impressed by the article and enjoyed her new knowledge gained. Her father had obviously also read the article; his spectacles were found, *ex post facto,* lying on the G-spot article in *Sarie* ... At last, sexuality was becoming a subject that could even be discussed in magazines. The taboo was thawing, even if one needed spectacles to spot it.

EIGHT
Religious fervour ignored
1980–1989

THE APARTHEID GOVERNMENT RELIED heavily on the Bible for its policy of racial segregation. It often referred to itself as a Christian government and built concepts such as "Christian National Education" into the Education Act and stated Christian ideals as being at the heart of the Publications Act in section 1 of that Act. It was, accordingly, astounding for many Christians to find that as from 1980, the Appeal Board was not ordering the excision of the taking in vain of the Lord's Name in films with age restrictions and even, here and there, in films without age restrictions. The argument from religious quarters was that whatever the functional value of such language in a film or play, it could never be accepted. However, we were arguing with legal substantiation that "offensive" had a restricted legal meaning and that only the most repugnant instances could be cut legitimately. What was blasphemous to the Judaeo-Christian view was not necessarily blasphemous or offensive in law.

In the film comedy *Back to School*, released in 1986, the father of one of the students, who returns to study at College to inspire his son, opens a door to find a beautiful college girl showering. He exclaims (and this was hilarious): "Jesus!". To have cut the word in this non-restricted film would have been absurd. There was not the slightest indication that he intended to be blasphemous. And who could cut the typical English middle-class *Shirley Valentine*'s profanities, against the background of her great sense of humour? There were many more examples. The reality that many people speak in this manner was accepted.

Nevertheless, even today, many viewers do not accept the approach of the Films and Publications Board and the Broadcasting Complaints Commission. They still believe that no dramatic value can trump the Ten Commandments, which forbid such use in absolute terms. Before such language could be cut in an age-restricted film, it must however when judged in context, amount to the scandalising of God. This is a very lenient test. The result was that the three* books in Afrikaans that were banned in the pre-1980 years as being offensive to religious Christian feelings were all unbanned early in the eighties. Earlier, with me as acting chairman in 1976, we passed Joseph Heller's *Catch 22*, in which profanity and crude language formed part of the hilarious satire. One often hears people refer to a catch-22 situation; is it always understood? Of course, it had to do with the clause in the US Army's contract that gave a soldier three weeks' leave, unless cancelled by the army! This was a bit like censorship in the old days: you had freedom of expression, unless "cancelled" by the authorities.

Currently, section 16(2)(c) of the Constitution has a more tolerant test: the advocacy of hatred based on religion which amounts to incitement to cause harm.† This test was also introduced by the

---

*   *Looking on Darkness, Magersfontein* and *Donderdag of Woensdag.*

†   See sections 16(4)(a)(ii) and 18(3)(a)(ii) of the Films and Publications Act, No 65 of 1996 and clause 4.2 (previously 16.3) of the Broadcasting Code (see www.bccsa.co.za). The Act, as does the Code, exempts bona fide drama, art and science.

1994 Task Group and Parliament accepted it in the new Films and Publications Act of 1996. It is also the test applied by the Broadcasting Complaints Commission and the Complaints and Compliance Committee of the Independent Communications Authority of South Africa today. I must admit that I also chaired the drafting of the Code applied by the two bodies mentioned. But, to my mind, there is no alternative constitutional approach. If the language does not amount to hate speech as defined in the Constitution, it may not be forbidden. Even the legal definition of blasphemy will have to be adapted to section 16(2)(c) of the Constitution.* I will argue in a later chapter that the violation of religious dignity of a person is not sufficient. Three elements must be present: (1) advocacy of hatred that constitutes (2) incitement to (3) harm (which could be a serious invasion of dignity).

A BOOK WHICH CAUSED CONTROVERSY worldwide, Salman Rushdie's *The Satanic Verses*, was submitted by Penguin Books for consideration by a publications committee in 1988. A publications committee found it to be offensive to the religious convictions or feelings of the Muslim section of the population. Penguin Books lodged an appeal to the Appeal Board. We received copies for our consideration on appeal. I started reading the novel and must confess that the pace was so slow that I fell asleep ever so often while reading it. What the outcome of the appeal would have been remains open: Penguin Books, obviously as a result of the *Fatwa* declared in 1989 against Salman Rushdie, decided to withdraw the appeal.

---

* In accordance with section 39 of the Constitution.

The current Films and Publications Board published a notice stating that the book was no longer on the banned list – basing this on the fact that there was a new Act. This notice was, with respect, not supported by the new Act. The Act of 1996 expressly provides that works that were banned under the previous Acts remained banned until an application for reconsideration is lodged with the new Board. Many complaints were received from Muslim quarters. The Board then decided to reconsider the matter. The reasoning of the Board is historically important and I quote it in full in Addendum Two to this book.

Firstly, one has to accept that the first decision of the new Board was a nullity for the introductory reasons stated; otherwise the Board could not have inquired into the matter again in June 2000. The reasons quoted in the addendum must, accordingly, be regarded as the first valid decision of the Board after the new Act had become fully operational in July 1998. The status quo was that the distribution of the book was prohibited under the Act of 1974 and that it remained prohibited until set free, on application, under the new Act. There was no possession ban of the book under the Act of 1974.

As appears from the Board's reasoning, the Board in the first instance held that the book did not amount to the advocacy of hatred towards Islam. This is the test which is prescribed in the Act. Furthermore, the Board regarded the book as bona fide literature. However, acting in terms of section 36 of the Constitution, it limited the distribution to higher education libraries and stated that persons were free to import and possess the book.

All this was brought about by modifying the X18 limitation which, according to the Act, is a limitation that may be imposed on publications and films which predominantly contain *sexually* explicit material. These publications and films may only be distributed from licensed premises to persons older than 18. It does not pertain to *religion* but only to soft pornography and a tribunal, such as the Board, is not permitted to widen its powers.

Let me at the outset say that the decision of the Board was a wise one, given the strong feelings of Muslims against the book. But did the Board truly lift the restriction and if so, to what extent? Except in the case of child pornography, any publication classified as XX (that is, banned for distribution) by the Board, may be imported and possessed. If a person hands a copy to a friend, it does not amount to "distribution".* The very limited distribution to and by deposit libraries and some higher education libraries is the only change which was brought about by the Board, and this could have been done by way of an exemption by the Board's Executive in terms of section 22 of the Act, even if the novel had remained banned.

Accordingly, my view is that effectively the novel has remained banned for distribution. Free distribution is what the Act is about, not distribution by way of exemption. Legally the book is free. In practice it remains prohibited, except for scholars. Once again, a wise decision given the sensitivities involved.

ANOTHER ISSUE RELATING TO ISLAM comes to mind. In 1984 the Islamic Centre in Durban published a booklet titled *Crucifixion or Crucifiction?* The booklet launched an attack on the manner in which

---

*   *S v Ravan Press (Pty) Ltd & Others* 1976(1) SA 929(T).

Christians believed in Jesus and put forward that aspects of that belief were in fact blasphemous. One of the very critical points raised was how a Christian could believe that God would allow his Son to be crucified. This caused an outcry amongst many Christians and the booklet was banned as offensive to Christians. An appeal was lodged with the Appeal Board. The later Chief Justice, Ismail Mahomed SC, appeared for the Centre.

Before the hearing, Mahomed SC approached me in Chambers and objected that the persons who were sitting on the appeal were all Christians and that the hearing would, accordingly, be perceived to be unfair. He had hardly completed his sentence when Moulana Jeena from the Transvaal Jamiat-Ul-Ulama entered my chambers – I had co-opted him for the hearing. Mahomed SC immediately withdrew his objection and expressed his admiration for the decision to include a prominent member of the Muslim community on the Board. On several occasions after that the later Chief Justice would kindly recall this step as a sign of true fairness in a time when apartheid was still very much alive.

At the hearing, Mahomed SC argued that the booklet, although outspoken, remained within the realm of what was permitted by freedom of religion and freedom of speech. His oratory was magnificent and the argument brilliant, as was customary for this admirable lawyer. To illustrate his brilliance, the following recollection comes to mind: Appeal Board member, Mr Fuchs, well known to the reader by now, who was also famous for his eloquent oratory, suddenly asked during the hearing: "But Mr Mahomed, what would you say if someone of the ilk of George Bernard Shaw were to make remarks against Muslims which were, in this publication, made against Christians?" The immediate and brilliant answer was (of course, tongue-in-cheek): "Mr Fuchs, if that were ever to have been said by a man of the genius of George Bernard Shaw, which I deny, I might give the matter a second thought!" Mr Fuchs was silent after that: one genius's respect for another genius. We upheld the appeal against the ban and set the booklet free for distribution.

A Christian delegation that came to see me after the ban was lifted, could not be convinced that our judgment was correct in law. But such is the path of censorship: there is seldom consensus and the persons who believe that they have been wronged, would often resort to sensational propaganda. The road of innovation and transformation is mostly a lonely road.

In 1983 we approved *Jesus Christ Superstar,* by way of a majority vote, with one cut* and subject to an age restriction of 16. By this time it had been banned in 1975 and also by the Appeal Board in 1981. However, a ban could be reconsidered on application after two years. The 1983 Committee of Experts had advised very positively on the film and a publications committee in Cape Town had also approved it. I was astounded by the reaction that most of my colleagues now had to the film. They† were enthusiastic about the message of the film and were struck by scenes of torture of Jesus and the crucifixion. The rock music had also somehow lost its ini-

---

*   The Gethsemane song was shortened a little. It was regarded as offen-
sively disrespectful to God the Father. When the SABC broadcast the
film in the 1980s, no cuts were made and the Broadcasting Complaints
Commission dismissed all complaints.

†   Douglas Fuchs (earlier Director General of the SABC) and Piet van der
Merwe, a Dutch Reformed Minister, were close to tears.

tial effect, which had been disturbing to many Christians who reasoned that the film had changed Jesus into a rock star. Time would,
by 1983, seem to have removed the "rock" effect. It was realised, for
the first time, that this medium could be used with great success to
improve the understanding of Jesus amongst non-believers and even,
some believers. Prof. Johan Heyns, who was vehemently criticised
by his colleagues for testifying in favour of the film in 1975, was
vindicated.

It was also of interest that a publications committee with a church
minister, Dr Piet Bingle, as its chairman had now approved the film
at the first level. I will never forget the words in the committee's
reasoning: "May the Lord's blessing be with this film." A good example of how time provides a different perspective.

Years later I was astounded (and impressed) to hear the CD of
the rock opera as background music to a party held by one of my
rather conservative friends. "What a lovely song", someone remarked
of Mary Magdalene's well-known – earlier very controversial –
song about her spiritual love for Jesus. The earlier conservative and
incorrect interpretation was that she had implied sexual love.

A JEHOVAH WITNESS ISSUE OF *The Watchtower*, was banned in 1982 by
a committee since it rejected the Trinity. The Jehovah Witnesses
indeed reject the Trinity as part of their faith. Yet, the committee
banned the distribution since it was in conflict with section 1 of the
Act, which stipulated that Christian principles must be applied in
the execution of the Act. The committee did not realise that freedom of religion was part of our common law and that the Act most
definitely permitted the coexistence of other religions with the

Christian religion in South Africa. As I had done before, on the filing of an appeal, I set aside the ban pending the outcome of the Board's decision. The Board set aside the ban.

NOW THAT DAN BROWN'S *THE DA VINCI CODE* has been such a bestseller, the drama surrounding the 1982 publishing of a sensational review of Baigent and Leigh's *Holy Blood Holy Grail* in a popular magazine, *Scope*, comes to mind. The authors of the book claimed that Jesus had not died on the cross, that He had been married and that his descendants had been traced in France. Action Moral Standards was up in arms and filed complaints with the Directorate. This was headline news in newspapers.

When the matter reached the Appeal Board, it held the sensational manner in which the matter was dealt with in *Scope* to have been offensive to the religious convictions or feelings of the Christian section of the populace. However, the book itself was not found to be undesirable by the Appeal Board; it formed part of legitimate debate on religion.

Looking back I believe that the Appeal Board should not have reacted that strongly to the *Scope* review, despite the sensational treatment. Freedom of speech requires that even the offensive be published at times. Of course, almost 31 years have gone by and many Christians have developed a much more tolerant attitude to debate, even on crucial issues. Yet, the debate amongst scholars is still substantial on matters such as the virgin birth of Jesus and Jesus's ascension from the grave. Nevertheless, the vast majority of Christians are not even prepared to discuss the historical veracity of the traditional views in this regard – an approach I find saddening within the new paradigm of freedom of expression. What we need is more discussion, not "prohibition"!

IN 1980 THE BOARD WAS CONFRONTED with a number of challenges: would we, for the first time in the censorship history of South Africa, permit the taking in vain of the Lord's Name in films such as *Kramer vs. Kramer* and the many "fucks" (used in a secondary sense) in Coppola's *Apocalypse Now?* We rose to the challenge and allowed them on the basis of the dramatic function of the words. Then came *Raging Bull*, a film about a boxer who constantly used the f-words, then the biography of a stand-up comic, *Lenny*, and by then – as colleague Kotie de Jager put it – the words had gained official recognition. Following this, it became practice to allow the words, and the test became whether a crude or profane word was used repugnantly and not necessarily whether it was functional. Ultimately, almost all instances where this word was uttered were allowed in mature films.

The taking in vain of the Lord's Name does not, as such, amount to blasphemy in law. The words, judged contextually, must be used in a manner which scandalises God before such a finding can be made. The debate about this matter is still very real at the time of publication of this book. However, the official bodies involved in films, the Films and Publications Board and the Broadcasting Complaints Commission do not regard the taking in vain of the Lord's Name as hate speech. According to these bodies, age restrictions and classifications take care of the problem. In a constitutional democracy the question is, however, what the Constitution permits: the Constitution prohibits hate speech and it is clear that the taking in vain of the Lord's Name would, only in the most exceptional circumstances, meet the hate-speech test.

The debates continued throughout the eighties. To what extent would it be permissible to allow crude combinations between the taking in vain of the Lord's Name and crudities such as "fuck"? Bearing in mind the words are being used to emphasise astonishment, surprise or agony and not directed at demeaning Jesus. When a character acted by Tom Cruise arrived in Vietnam in *Born on the Fourth of July* (1989) and combined profanity and "fuck" in the crudest of forms to express his disgust at the bodies of massacred children strewn over the scene, we held the expression to be not undesirable.

Johann van der Westhuizen, the human rights lawyer and current Constitutional Court Justice, acting for United International Pictures (UIP), together with Gerald Sobel from UIP, have persistently during the preceding seven years been opposing, with substantial success, each cut of a crude or profane word as ordered by the committees at first level. Even the extremely crude and profane army language of the sergeant major in *Full Metal Jacket* made the cut by 1988 – with an age restriction of 2-19. Robert Howie and Bill Sharp from Ster-Kinekor were equally ardent in their appeals in this and other respects.

A FILM WHICH CAUSED US AN UNBELIEVABLE amount of trouble was Monty Python's *The Life of Brian*. The film was nothing less than a skit on the grand Hollywood sagas of the life of Jesus and the Apostles. Brian is also born in Bethlehem and he is mistaken by all and sundry for Jesus: the Wise Men from the East turn up with presents at Brian's birthplace and his mother (played by one of the male members of the Monty Python team) tells them to scram; and this confusion continues throughout the film. A theologian who testified before the Board stated that even if it be accepted that Brian is a person different from Jesus – as is clear from the film – the reason why viewers laugh is because they relate what happens to Brian to what is related in the Bible happened to Jesus. Our Committee of Experts, chaired by the well-known film critic Danie du Toit, advised that the film was not aimed at denigrating Jesus, but at poking fun at people who readily find a "redeemer" and then blindly follow him. We decided to permit the film to be screened at a Norwood theatre in the suburbs of Johannesburg where art films and the like were usually screened. An outcry from Action Moral Standards followed.

Since we would have had to consider further theatres for its screening, I decided to invite Eddie van Zyl, the Executive Director of the Action group, to testify before us. He told us that he had met "old" Monty Python in London and that "Monty" was intent upon denigrating everything that a Christian holds dear. Johann van der Westhuizen, acting for UIP, cross-examined him on his visit to "Monty Python", which was of course not a person but a group. A few months later we permitted the film to be screened in Johannesburg at a mid-city theatre with a month's running time. Again the complaints flooded in. Of course once again, the complaints almost never came from people who had actually seen the film, but from persons who were part of a campaign obviously organised by Action Moral Standards.

BY 1989 I HAD GAINED THE TRUST of many journalists from the four major media houses. I permitted them to watch movies on appeal with us – thereby ensuring that they remain informed. I had also made a point of regularly dining with the reporters on the censorship trail since 1980. This provided a useful contact with what was happening at ground level. Charlene Smith from the *Sunday Express,* one of my reporter friends, argued, I understand, my integrity in anticensorship quarters. Journalists such as Kym Hamilton, Paul Boekkooi, Ruda Landman, Sue Leeman, Keith Abendroth, Rina Minervini, Barrie Ronge, Mariechen Waldner, Philip de Bruin, Dewald Joubert, Charlene Smith and Peter Sullivan, an editor, had come to understand that Rome was not built in a day. And this certainly also applied to censorship. By 1989 immense strides had been made both from an artistic and a political point of view. After I had suffered the agony of having passed *Cry Freedom!* in 1988 and the seizing of the film the next day by the Commissioner of Police, the media was most sympathetic, praising the Board for its independence.

When the film *The Last Temptation of Christ* was not approved by a committee in Cape Town and we confirmed that decision in 1989 on appeal, the media was again very understanding. The *Pretoria News* expressed its sadness at the decision, but empathised with the dilemma we found ourselves in. I had invited a number of journalists and editors – amongst them Peter Sullivan of the Argus Group – to view the film with us. Here was a film, extremely well made, which broke away completely from the Gospel's rendition of what happened on the cross. Jesus is shown to be, finally, tempted to leave the cross in a flight of imagination and to marry Mary Magdalene. After she and the child she was expecting die, Jesus weds Maria, the sister of Lazarus and Martha. The film was all but a cheap attempt at degrading Christ. Our Committee of Experts praised the film for its depth. However, we believed that the test of "offensiveness" in terms of the Act of 1974 had been met and acted accordingly.

To illustrate the immense emotions of many Christians about this film, a recounting of the following incident would suffice. The Directorate of Publications had in 1992, after I was no longer the chairman of the Appeal Board, exempted the film for a film festival in Johannesburg. Activist Christians had almost bought out the one show and had entered the cinema and some of them lay across the empty seats so that no one else could take a seat. The police were called in. On the advice of one of the organisers, I was telephoned

at midnight to explain. I confirmed that the Directorate had granted an exemption. The next day the exemption was withdrawn. An application to the Supreme Court against the withdrawal failed.

In 1999 the new Films and Publications Board approved the video version of *The Last Temptation of Christ*. There was an outcry from Christians and hundreds of letters were received by the then Chief Executive of the Board, Dr Makaula. Classification of the cinema version was accordingly not granted. However, the Act does not permit such a distinction. It does not differentiate between the different formats in which a film is released as did the Act of 1974. When chairing the Task Group which drafted the new Act, we then decided that the distinction between different formats would no longer apply. There was no manner in which the distinction could be justified legally. The Films and Publications Act of 1996 exempted drama. Whatever one could say against the film, it could not be argued cogently that it was not bona fide drama. The Committee of Experts had in 1989 already regarded it as such.

The matter became academic when the Hollywood distributors of the film decided in 2000 to withdraw the distribution of both the film and the video. The pending appeal against the decision of the Board not to permit the cinema distribution was, accordingly, withdrawn by Anant Singh, the acclaimed South African film producer, and his brother Sanjeev Singh. I had been briefed to argue the case on their behalf on appeal and had already prepared documentation for the appeal to the Review Board.

In 2007, etv broadcast the film at 23:15 with an age restriction and classification. Once again there was an outcry. The Broadcasting Complaints Commission (BCCSA) received more than 1200 obviously orchestrated complaints. The Registrar accepted a complaint from the Wesleyan Church and the BCCSA, by way of a majority vote, held the broadcast to have been in contravention of the Broadcasting Code.* The majority of the members, held that the film did not amount to bona fide drama since the producer must have known that it would offend millions of Christians. I filed a minority opinion. Although conceding that the film could possibly still be held to be offensive, it was argued that offensiveness was no longer a ground for limiting free speech. The constitutional test was now whether the film amounts to hate speech based on religion. The conclusion was that the film did not amount to hate speech and was a drama which adults deserved to see for themselves if they chose to do so. On appeal to a second Tribunal of the BCCSA, the approach of the majority was not upheld. The reasoning was that Jesus had, also in this instance, not given in to the temptation.

Fervour was, however, brewing in an even more acute area: state security. This ultimately led to a clash between the Appeal Board and the Commissioner of Police with which I deal in the next chapter.

---

*   Read the judgment of my respected colleague, Prof. Henning Viljoen on the BCCSA website: www. bccsa.co.za.

NINE

Security and the voice of the majority
1979–1990

THE VAST MAJORITY OF APARTHEID SUPPORTERS had an immense sympathy and respect for the dignity of the police and of the apartheid establishment. Consequently, any book, play or film which criticised the police in their treatment of black people was under suspicion. Jack Cope's *The Dawn Comes Twice* was banned by the Appeal Board in 1977 because it included fictional unlawful acts by the police. To me this amounted to an unacceptable limitation on freedom of speech. It was extremely doubtful whether these acts posed a risk to the public order or the security of the state, as required by the Publications Act. How could the police be sacrosanct when reality contradicted this? One needs to only page through the reports of the Truth and Reconciliation Commission to come to a different conclusion. Of course it would be wrong to categorically blame each policeman. But the task the police were given under apartheid legislation – as is the case in all oppressive regimes – was open to abuse. Books and films should address this critically, whether it be by way of a documentary or fiction.

When I took over in 1979 as acting chairman, the first signs of a new, freedom-oriented, dispensation were already in the air: we unbanned Nadine Gordimer's *Burger's Daughter* which was said to have been a risk to the security of the state. How such an intricate novel could ever be regarded as a risk to security remains a riddle to me!* Of course, it sympathised with the cause of the disenfranchised majority. But that could never be a reason to ban a book. *The Dawn Comes Twice* was also unbanned in the eighties, as were many other books with similar and much more problematic content.

One of the criteria in terms of the Act of 1974 was that when a publication or film brought a section of the population into contempt it was deemed to be undesirable. Although this is a form of hate speech, it went much further than what our Constitution currently regards as hate speech. When *The Covenant* by James Michener was found to be in contravention of this criterion by a publications committee in 1981, I realised how sensitive (and irrational) traditional pro-apartheid feelings were. It is true that the novel questioned the very roots of the Afrikaner in so far as the covenant of 1838 was concerned. The covenant constituted a promise to God that if He granted victory over the Zulus to a Voortrekker commando led by Andries Pretorius, they and their descendants undertook to regard 16 December as a Sunday and to build a church to commemorate this day. A hundred years later in 1938, a grand symbolical trek was organised from all corners of the country to Pretoria. The foundation stone of the Voortrekker Monument in Pretoria was laid and nationalism amongst Afrikaners reached a climax. In a sense the monument for many Afrikaners also symbolised the triumph of the Afrikaner under the guidance of God. In the centre of the monument there is a sarcophagus with the in-

---

*   Prof. Peter Tittlestad, chairman of an advisory committee, expressed a similar view in his report to the Appeal Board.

scription: "We for thee South Africa". Words that formed part of the national anthem before 1994. This rise of Afrikaner nationalism contributed to the National Party's victory at the general election in 1948 and to the foundations of apartheid instituted by that government.

The Covenant questioned the integrity of the Afrikaner in its 1838 covenant with God and also sharply criticised its policy of apartheid. The novel had hardly been banned when the local distributors filed an appeal. Within a week I suspended the ban pending the outcome of the appeal. I simply could not believe that a Michener novel could be banned. A publications committee also soon afterwards banned an issue of *Reader's Digest* in which an abridged version of the book appeared. Once again, within a day after the appeal was lodged, I suspended the ban pending the outcome of an appeal. How despotic could censorship get? I was shocked by this demonstration of unreasonableness. Something had to be done to move South Africa out of the grip of fundamentalism.

Although the Appeal Board agreed that the novel was not that well researched and that it gave a view of the Afrikaner that was not that well informed either, this was most certainly no justification for a ban on the distribution of the novel in South Africa. What had become of freedom of expression? Fairness or truth of speech was not a requirement under the Publications Act, unless the material, judged as a whole, also fell within the criteria spelt out in section 47(2) of the Act. Surely much more than absence of fairness or truth was required by the subsection; the book was not a newspaper, where such rules applied, and still apply, according to the Press Code. *The Covenant* was removed from the banned list after a hearing before the Appeal Board. I could feel the first signs of personal revulsion against the suffocating system, which could even ban a Michener novel.

A CRUCIAL PROBLEM CONFRONTING Director Braam Coetzee* in 1980 was the long list of banned books, newspapers, articles and pamphlets written and published by black authors and democracy-oriented publishers. These included material that demanded a new unitary state with a vote for all its citizens, some that called for the release of Nelson Mandela from prison, others that demanded that detention without trial for the "enemies" of the state be put to an end, printed material that decried the moving of black and coloured communities without their consent, articles that damned the way in which the police were crushing the voice of the majority and, yes, published photos of police brutality towards black people, for example in the newspaper *New Nation*, with Zwelakhe Sisulu as its editor.

John Dugard, from the Centre for Applied Legal studies (Wits) assisted me in 1983 in setting up a private meeting with Prof. Es'kia Mphahlele from Wits. I managed to also convince Prof. Nkabinde, rector of the University of Zululand, to attend. The advice was clear: African literature and newspapers posed no real risk to security and the voice of the majority needed to be heard so as to ensure that the suppressed voice would not be pushed into revolution and violence.

My own view was much clearer after this meaningful meeting: only when material posed an actual danger of violence or amounted

---

*   Director of Publications 1980–1997.

to a real contribution to violence, would we ban the distribution. And this was seldom the case. *Staffrider, Learn and Teach* and many other voices of deep anger against the apartheid regime were unbanned by the Appeal Board. We also approved Sipho Sepamla's *A Ride on the Whirlwind*, a novel which included appalling conduct by the police in Soweto.* A few months later I was invited to lunch at Wits. Sipho (admirably) attended the lunch, whilst a white lecturer had, I understood, declined the invitation to eat with a censor, even if he was bringing about change towards freedom of expression.

IN SO FAR AS COMMUNIST LITERATURE was concerned, all the books of Marx, Lenin, Trotsky, Stalin and the like were banned – even for possession. Only by way of special exemption were they permitted to be kept under lock in certain research libraries. This was an unnecessary limitation on the necessity for research. In 1983 we appointed Prof. Gerrit Olivier (who later in the 1990s became our first Ambassador to Russia) and Prof. Marthinus Vorster, head of the Department of Public Law at the University of Pretoria, to advise the Board. Their advice was clear: the possession ban on the works was creating an unnecessary limitation on research in the field of communism and related fields. Their report led to the

---

*   *Wikipedia* summarises the life of this splendid person as follows: "Sydney Sipho Sepamla (1932–2007) was a contemporary South African poet and novelist. Born in a township near Krugersdorp, Sipho Sepamla lived most of his life in Soweto. He studied teaching at Pretoria Normal College and published his first volume of poetry, *Hurry Up to It!*, in 1975. During this period he was active in the Black Consciousness movement and his 1977 book *The Soweto I Love*, partly a response to the Soweto Riots, was banned by the apartheid regime ..."

unbanning of the possession of such works and later the distribution bans were also lifted.

ANDRÉ BRINK'S COMMENT IN THE mid-1980s after the tide of unbannings had commenced, was more or less as follows: Van Rooyen was giving censorship a good name – a matter of concern.* There was also an article by J.M. Coetzee, the 2003 Nobel Prize Laureate for Literature, in the late eighties referring to me as a civil servant (which I was not!) and that censorship was based on fear. Of course I felt compelled to write a letter to him explaining that I held judicial office and that I was not a civil servant. But I did mention to him that I agreed that censorship was mostly based on fear. He kindly replied and apologised for the error in having called me a civil servant.

EARLY IN THE EIGHTIES WE LIFTED THE BAN on posters which promoted the "Release Mandela" campaign. Why could people not agitate for the release of a leader – should they not at least have that right? Board member Piet van der Merwe reminded us of similar demands for the release of Gen. De Wet† and Jopie Fourie‡ – rebels

---

*   I should add that André Brink gave me his full support for the new Films and Publications Act, which exempted bona fide literature from the banning powers of the new Board. The accent in the new Act would be on protection of children.

†   De Wet was the renowned guerilla hero of the Anglo-Boer War and wrote a significant book on this kind of warfare. He was released.

‡   Jopie Fourie was not released but shot after a (questionable) military trial.

against the government's involvement in the war against Germany in South West Africa during World War I. The posters did not, in any manner, promote violence but demanded what was reasonable. Later in the eighties we also, on appeal, unbanned a calendar which reminded possessors of important days of remembrance for the ANC. I will always be grateful to Justice Richard Goldstone – later a Judge of the first Constitutional Court and the leading prosecutor at the time of the newly constituted International Criminal Tribunal – for approving our approach to security matters in a judgment of the High Court. He rejected the state's argument that such a calendar was a security risk. Our approach was closely related to the approach of the American courts: there had to be a clear and real danger before a publication or a film was a security risk. We were not prepared to add that the danger also had to be a "present" danger. But Christof Heyns, in his 1992 doctoral thesis on Conscientious Objection, has argued that in effect we were applying the American doctrine. Looking back, I tend to agree with him.

THE SECURITY PUBLICATIONS COMMITTEE, appointed by the Directorate of Publications, differed strongly from the new approach. One of the comments was: "The Appeal Board is clearly out of touch. We are not bound to follow them. The tail is wagging the dog!" This statement was rejected by the Appeal Board. Although each set of facts had to be decided on its own merits, the Appeal Board *interpreted* the Act and the committees were bound to follow that interpretation: the Board was not merely a *tail*. If the committees declined to follow our guidelines, the Directorate of Publications was bound to appeal so as to ensure consistency. The Directorate constantly appealed where it felt that our guidelines had been departed from. I am proud to say that Director Braam Coetzee personally supported our security approach. It was certainly valuable to have his support and looking back, I am delighted that we followed this open approach, despite all the opposition from government quarters. Hugo Malherbe, the deputy chairman, also gave his full support to the new approach. John Dugard's Centre for Applied Legal Studies also took steps to apply for the reconsideration of publications banned in the past. This, at least, assisted us in our approach and led to some decrease in the long list of banned books, some originating from before 1980, when our terms commenced.

Conversely an ex-Commissioner of Police on the Board, General Gideon Joubert, put forward the other side of the coin and warned of impending disaster: "I must tell you, Pink Floyd's song, 'The Wall', will teach thousands of would-be black revolutionaries to remove the bricks from the wall and we, the whites, are those bricks." A little later, early in the eighties, the same general warned: "When the revolution moves to the cities, we have had it." He was particularly concerned about the spreading of propaganda which supported the cause of the disenfranchised majority. The argument was that this would give false hope to black people and that they would then choose the only alternative: violence. So as not to characterise the General as a difficult colleague, I should add that he was a splendidly mannered and good-natured man. My view, as substantiated by Proff. Mphahlele and Nkabinde as well as the well-argued cases by advocates such as Gilbert Marcus, John Dugard, Edwin Cameron, Lauren Jacobson, Kathy Satchwell, the late Etienne Mureinik, Johann van der Westhuizen and Nic Haysom was, however, that the harsher we reacted to publications, the more other alternatives such as violence, would become inevitable. This view was shared by the majority of the Board, which had by 1985, at my insistence with Minister F.W. de Klerk, been joined by three members of the majority population, who were not permitted to take part in any elections: Prof. A.L. Mawasha, Rev. J.J. Mettler and Mr A. Ramsamy. At the Appeal Board they could, at least, vote ...

Desmond Abernethy, the well-known former principal of Boys High in Pretoria also represented a strong voice for more freedom after he joined the Board in 1977. Lynda Gilfillan, who had joined the Board in 1986 and was, at the time, a lecturer in English at the University of Pretoria, also supported this approach.

The liberty-oriented policy of the Board led to a substantial reduction by 1986 in the number of publications submitted by the Security Police to the Directorate. I was told by Director Braam Coetzee that the Security Police had, as it were, given up on us. This approach was probably accentuated by the cross-examination before the Appeal Board of Colonel Horak from the Security Police by Gilbert Marcus. The state had called the colonel as an expert witness to support the view that the black media posed a security risk. The cross-examination led to the colonel having had to concede that he was not a specialist in communications and had not read the most prominent works in this field. I had some understanding for the efforts of the colonel who was doing his job, but I agreed with the view put forward by Gilbert Marcus: freedom of expression was also a mechanism to ensure that people who could not vote would have some avenue to let their voice be heard. A voice that demanded equality and democracy for all South Africans.

BUT ALLOW ME TO TAKE A FEW STEPS BACK. By 1984 the *Freedom Charter** was being distributed (unlawfully) on a much wider scale than before. The matter of the ban on its possession came before us. I decided to appoint Gilbert Marcus, who was associated with the Centre for Human Rights Studies at Wits, to address the Board on whether its distribution was likely to pose a risk to the security of the apartheid state. Gilbert had been arguing a number of appeals before us and had gained special expertise in security matters. When I phoned Gilbert to ask him whether he would be prepared to act as *amicus curiae*, his response was: "I'll jump at the opportunity!"

He rightly contended in a well-prepared argument before the Board, that as it stood the *Charter* was a mere Bill of Rights which demanded what a Bill of Rights would demand: equality, the rule of law, the vote for all citizens and equal opportunities for all. Of course, the rights demanded conflicted directly with government policy. However, there was no sign of the propagation of violence in the *Charter* itself. If the document was used to incite violence, then that had nothing to do with the Appeal Board, which could only adjudicate within the four corners of the *Charter* before it. We decided not to confirm the possession ban proposed by the Committee.

A day or two later, two members of the Security Police (a colonel and a brigadier) came to see me unannounced at my chambers. They introduced themselves by stating that the Commissioner of Police, Gen. Coetzee, conveyed his compliments. They had in some way or another been informed that we had declined to confirm the possession ban. They were particularly concerned. At a stage, the

---

*   The Bill of Rights that the ANC drafted at Kliptown in 1955.

colonel said: "But why did you appoint a communist to advise you in unbanning the *Freedom Charter?*" I first rejected their assertion as to communism (persons who differed from apartheid policy were often, at the time, referred to loosely as "communists" by supporters of the regime) and then explained to them that the Appeal Board had found no sign of the advocacy of violence in the *Freedom Charter* as such and that we were not permitted to consider the intention behind a publication. I further explained that if anyone misused a publication, that was not the concern of the Board. The brigadier agreed with me. The colonel remained unconvinced. I also told the colonel that Gilbert was not a communist and, indeed, a splendid advocate. I only mention this here because I informed Gilbert about this allegation in later years. He thought this was hilarious. Gilbert has become one of the most prominent senior

counsel that South Africa has seen and freedom of speech has remained an important part of his constitutional practice, which has become extremely busy. He often appears in the Constitutional Court and has also acted before the Broadcasting Complaints Commission.

What I found peculiar about this meeting with the security officers was how the information had reached the Security Police that we had unbanned the *Freedom Charter* the previous day. Was the news leaked by one of the members? I doubted that. On the other hand, Lauren Jacobsen, an eminent media lawyer, who often appeared before us for the publishers of novels, conveyed to me in the 1990s that she had a strong suspicion at the time that my phone was being tapped. She had heard suspicious sounds when phoning me, which did not emanate from her phone connection since she had detected the same sound when phoning me from elsewhere.

I was most considerate with my two visitors; not telling them that we were independent and that the questioning was totally unacceptable. On the other hand, their manners were also impeccable and they, of course, knew that security in this field lay within our sole jurisdiction. In 1994, as chairman of the Task Group, which drafted the new Films and Publications Act, I also consulted with the then Commissioner of Police, Johan van der Merwe. He was the brigadier who earlier had met with me on the *Freedom Charter* in the 1980s. He supported our approach that security within a new constitutional dispensation should be a matter for the courts and not an administrative body, such as the Films and Publications Board. We, accordingly, advised Parliament that the new Act of 1996 should not contain a security paragraph and this advice was accepted.

Shortly after my meeting with the two security officers in 1984, the opportunity arose for the Appeal Board to decide on a case where the distribution of the *Freedom Charter* had been prohibited by the so-called security committee of the Directorate of Publications. Once again we set that decision aside. Now the *Charter* could be possessed and distributed freely. After this the *Charter* was often published in newspapers and as a separate document. It was interesting to watch the role of the *Charter* as an unbanned document. It could now form part of the debate on a new South Africa: a debate which would not, from the government's side, have any significant effect before F. W. de Klerk became State President. The late 1980s was overshadowed by the debate between State President Botha and the imprisoned Nelson Mandela. State President Botha was demanding that Nelson Mandela should first undertake to abandon violence as a mechanism to change before he could be released. However, Nelson Mandela was not prepared to, as it were, barter for his freedom. His release would have to be unconditional and was, ultimately, unconditional when F. W. de Klerk ordered his release in February 1990.

AFTER THE UNBANNING OF THE *Freedom Charter* I received two important invitations: one from the State Department in the US and one from the British Foreign Office. In 1984 my wife, Martha, and I spent a month in the United States. I had the privilege of meeting with prominent freedom-of-speech experts, notably the top broadcasting expert Erwin Krasnow in Washington DC and the renowned Floyd Abrams in New York, who had won the Nixon tapes' case for the *New York Times* in the Supreme Court of the US. These meetings led to a treasured friendship with the two gentlemen – both were later also guests of mine in South Africa.

The next year in the UK, I had more than 35 meetings with persons who had different views about media controls, including the conservative campaigner against violence and indecency on TV, Mary Whitehouse. My wife and I met her for tea and sandwiches at the magnificent Ritz Hotel. What I found interesting about Mary Whitehouse was that she strongly emphasised the protection of children and was, for example, not against mere nudity in mature films. Her approach was accordingly not absolutist, as was that of South African conservative campaigners. What I found most informative were meetings with editors of the printed and broadcasting media. Their criticism of apartheid was vehement.

After the two trips I knew for sure that the apartheid regime could not last for much longer and that the Appeal Board was on the right path in the freeing of black political thought and expression, which would lead to democracy for all. Of course, the problem was that there were still other laws which prohibited the voice of the majority from being heard fully: detention without trial and the Emergency Regulations of the late 1980s are examples. And, of course, that voice was not in Parliament.

Although Director Braam Coetzee and I had splendid contact with our counterparts in other countries, notably Zimbabwe, England, Ireland, Norway, Australia and the USA, the pressure was also on some of them to cut ties with us. In 1984 we were invited to participate in an international conference on Film Classification in Toronto. James Ferman, the Director of the British Board of Film Classification, had organised the first such conference in London in 1980. As we were about to leave for Toronto, Braam and I were "dis-invited" – a word unknown to me at the time. We neverthe-less went to Toronto and our many friends, some from England and Norway, daily brought us copies of papers read during the day at the conference. The reason for the "dis-invitation" was criticism in the Toronto press against the Toronto Film Classification Board which was planning to introduce controls on video distribution. Braam had spoken to the Director who was instructed to "dis-invite" us: she was almost in tears ... However, any association with the dicta-torial South Africa provided ammunition to the critics in the Toronto press.

AN INTERESTING PROBLEM FROM NAMIBIA* presented itself in 1984. A publications committee had not only banned one issue of the Namibian newspaper, *Windhoek Observer*, but all future issues. At that time, Namibia still fell under our jurisdiction and only became independent in 1990. An appeal was immediately lodged with the Appeal Board, and Brian O'Linn SC, a future Judge in Namibia, argued the suspension of the ban pending the outcome of the ap-peal before me. Deon van Zyl SC, later to also become a Judge, argued the case for the publications committee. I suspended the ban pending the outcome of the appeal.

The complaint was that the newspaper was siding with SWAPO, which had an internal as well as an external wing and that we should ban the newspaper in the public interest. The external wing of SWAPO was waging a war with South Africa on the northern

---

*   Namibia was being governed by South Africa by way of an administra-tor general and his staff.

border of Namibia. The committee's reasons were based on what they perceived to be sympathy from the side of the newspaper with the plight of the external wing of SWAPO.

I was taken aback by attempts to influence the Board. We decided to continue with the case. The appeal was upheld. There was no sign in the issues of the *Windhoek Observer* that the cause of the enemy was being furthered by the newspaper. Had we confirmed the "all future issues" ban, I would have lost all hope that we were on the way to more freedom at the Appeal Board. Since the matter was urgent, colleague Kotie de Jager and I wrote the judgment into the early hours of the next morning. The camaraderie between the members of the Board was outstanding.

The evening after we had lifted the ban, someone who must have been involved in the complaint phoned me. Without wishing to be melodramatic, I believe that the following incident illustrates the strain under which we often worked. As the phone rang, the automatic light switch on the second floor of the building in which our offices were housed in Pretoria, hurled the floor into complete darkness with a loud bang. It was exactly 20:00 and the sudden loud noise gave me quite a fright in my isolated and lonely chambers. I felt around in the dark for the phone and when I heard a voice from Namibia enquiring as to what had happened, I pretended that I could not hear him. I was simply not ready or prepared to talk to him. When the phone rang again, I nevertheless answered and told him that we had lifted the ban. He was clearly distressed. He said that the State President would have to be approached to intervene. I told him that he was welcome to take the matter further, but that we were independent from government and would not take orders to ban a publication – not even from the

State President. In any case, why could the Namibian administration not take steps itself? It was clear that it would be much more acceptable within the Namibian political sphere if the blame could be placed on us for the ban. South Africa was fighting a war against the external wing of SWAPO and every means had to be employed to counter SWAPO.

I was delighted to hear that the *Windhoek Observer* was soon back to hitting out at the government in the interests of free speech and democracy.

I SHOULD ALSO MENTION OUR BAN on *Famous Dead Man*, a cabaret performed in a small theatre in Johannesburg. The play satirised Dr and Mrs Verwoerd.* It mocked all that was dear to Verwoerd supporters of the 1960s. We held the play to have amounted to a crude mixture of sex, politics and religion and offensive in terms of the Act. What we should have done was to have regarded it as political cabaret directed at a small likely audience – which made it innocuous. Of course, when one is involved in daily disputes, one is inclined to lose perspective. An attorney who had appeared before us in the matter, conceded that this was, in any case, the most problematic play that she had ever seen.

In October 2004 the Broadcasting Tribunal rejected a complaint

---

* Dr Verwoerd was the third Prime Minister after the National Party came to power in 1948. He succeeded Hans Strijdom in 1958 as Prime Minister and was assassinated in Parliament by the demented Dimitri Tsafendas, one of the ushers in Parliament, in September 1966. He was succeeded by John Vorster, who was then succeeded by P.W. Botha in 1980. The latter was the first executive State President. In 1988 F.W. de Klerk succeeded P.W. Botha.

of the Herstigte Nasionale Party (HNP)* against the SABC's broadcast of a play entitled *ID*. It also satirised Dr Verwoerd and how he was killed by Dimitri Tsafendas. At the end a black man dances for joy on the coffin of Dr Verwoerd and shouts "Amandla!"† The play, according to the HNP, amounted to hate speech against Afrikaners. The Tribunal held that the dignity of a deceased person is not protected in law. Political ideology is also not protected – in this case, that of the HNP. The complaint was not upheld.

AND THEN FOLLOWED THE DECLARATION of a state of emergency in 1987. I was asked by the Department of Home Affairs whether I could tighten the rules in regard to the so-called alternative media. I said that I could not do so, since I was bound by the Publications Act and also that I did not believe in any such tightening. At the Board it was argued on behalf of the State that the Appeal Board was bound to accept that a state of emergency had been declared and that it should, accordingly, apply stricter rules. The Board held unanimously that it was not bound by the state of emergency and that it would and should, itself, decide what the state of security is in relation to films and publications and whether the voice of the majority should not rather be heard in the interest of safety. We were praised for having taken this stand in the media. This was a feather in the cap of the Board and emphasised its independence.

---

* A conservative party which was formed during the prime minister term of John Vorster and which strived to have the principles of apartheid, as espoused by Dr Verwoerd, reinstated. This is still one of its aims as a political party today.

† The freedom cry of the African National Congress.

And that is the path we took. In fact, we regarded it as a risk to the security of the state to ban newspapers. To kill the voice of an editor and his journalists amounted to what must have and could have contributed to anger, which could have led to more violence. I thoroughly believed that there must be a newspaper outlet for suppressed feelings and ideals. Furthermore, the government had to hear and see how the suppressed majority felt. The suppression by the police state had to stop. It was in the interest of the security of the state to free Nelson Mandela and move into a new, democratic dispensation.

"FUCK THE REASONS IN YOUR JUDGMENT" the Minister of Home Affairs Stoffel Botha yelled at me over the phone in November 1987. "I have been planning to ban *New Nation* and *South* for three months under the Emergency Regulations and now you have *unbanned* them today under the Publications Act!" "Yes but …", I tried to explain that the Minister's decision and ours were under different legislative frameworks and that our decision would not affect his decision. But after another triple "fuck you", the phone was slammed down in my ear. I felt nauseous. I realised that it would of course have been a form of support for his decision the next week if he could say that the Board also had found the newspapers to be a risk for state security. But that was what the Board was not willing to do. We believed that a ban on the newspapers would be counterproductive. On the following Monday the Minister banned the papers for three months. At a meeting two weeks later the Minister had calmed down and apologised impliedly. Braam Coetzee, the Director of Publications was present. "But am I permitted in law to order you to take a stricter approach or intervene?" the Minister asked me. "No, sir, the Publications Act expressly prohibits anyone from influencing or attempting to influence the Appeal Board," I replied. "Then we have painted ourselves into a corner!" the Minister exclaimed. He told me he would seek senior opinion to check whether I was correct. I did not hear from him again.

However, thunderclouds were gathering over the Union Buildings, the seat of Government and the State Security Council. I could just imagine the heated debates about this Appeal Board which was not toeing the line. I could visualise the following dialogue:

"Is this Van Rooyen not a 'communist'? Who appointed this fool?"

"Well, Mr State President, you appointed him in 1980 and 1985 …"

"But he is bound by the Emergency Regulations!"

"Mr President, he has held that the Publications Act has priority over the Regulations and that the Appeal Board would, itself, decide what the limits of freedom based on security are."

I could well imagine the sense of utter despair and then of fury. The apartheid government did not countenance any opposition from any Board within the state structure; even if it were independent from the executive, as the Publications Appeal Board was by legislation.

In the meantime I was functioning with the full and justified conviction that we were independent, as the law guaranteed. And yet, that independence would soon be threatened, as I will describe in the next chapter.

TEN

Cry Freedom!
1988–1990

IN OCTOBER 1987 WE HEARD THAT Sir Richard Attenborough was producing a film called *Cry Freedom!* about Steve Biko, the black African Nationalist hero who had died as a result of wounds inflicted upon him in prison whilst being detained without trial in 1976. At that stage, Attenborough's huge success with the film *Ghandi* was cause for concern for the government. The Biko film could be as big a success and further worsen international relations for South Africa. A publications committee had found the film to be acceptable early in 1988 already. The Directorate did not appeal.

However, when it emerged that the film would be screened by United International Pictures at more than 30 cinemas on 29 July 1988, the Minister of Home Affairs referred the film to the Appeal Board on 25 July as he was entitled to do in terms of the Publications Act.

Piet van der Bijl SC (with Jacob Wessels) acted on behalf of the State and Johann van der Westhuizen (with Duard Kleyn) acted on behalf of the film distributors. Minister Botha, the then Minister of Home Affairs, invited me to his luxurious suite in the Post Office Building in Pretoria. He was extremely friendly. He suggested that I only appoint a Board of seven members. "Of course, you will have to have one black member on the Board, so as to show balance" the

Minister said. I ignored the obvious attempts at influencing the outcome of the matter and appointed all available members to sit with me. There were ten members on the Board for this case – three more than the quorum. I included the three black members.

This was to be a turning point in my life. The passing of the film would expose me to immense criticism from the apartheid government and would mean that I would not be reappointed as chairman eighteen months later. I also asked Prof. S.A. Strauss, who was an expert on the inquiry into the death of Steve Biko, to join us as an adviser. The outcome of that inquiry was that "no one could, in law, be held responsible for the death of the deceased". An outcry from antigovernment quarters followed, both nationally and internationally.

Before the hearing started, the international media conducted a short interview with me: cameras, microphones and journalist writing pads surrounded me in my chambers. "But are you independent?" one young lady asked (and, it was not the talented Christiane Amanpour!). "We *are* independent," I answered. I kept my promise and had to suffer personally for keeping that promise. But what is the sense of being a judicial officer if one does not have to live with the consequences of being independent? How this independence would be tested in the next few months I could simply not have foreseen.

The courtroom was packed. A well-known radio personality, Justus Tsungu, testified on behalf of the State that blood would flow on the streets if the film were to be screened. Prof. Pieter Fourie, a communications expert, explained the function of the scenes of violence and convincingly testified that they were not incitatory, but functional in showing the plight of a people who have been

oppressed. The film would rather lead to compassion than violence.

In a very strained three-hour meeting which followed the hearing, a majority of six to four members decided to make no cuts to
the film and pass it with an age restriction of 19.

The film included the terrible scenes where children were shot
by the police during the, by now, internationally known incident
when children, in their thousands, rose up against the apartheid
education system in Soweto in 1976. The scenes referred to were
extremely well produced and the viewer could feel the anger of the
thousands of protesting children. And then the (some say it was
unintended) shot from the gun of a policeman which, as it were,
threw the protest into pandemonium. Police officers were shoot-
ing at children and hitting them with sjamboks. The internationally known poster, where the body of Hector Peterson is carried,
was also realistically re-enacted in the film.

When writing the judgment I realised that the approval of the
film would change my life and future within the apartheid dispensation. I had worked on the judgment right through the night,
which was released to the national and international media at 09:00
on the 29th of July. The media was delighted. At last, a glimmer of
freedom!

I sat down in my chambers after both the national and international press had left and enjoyed a hamburger which my aides had
organised for me. The pressure seemed to be off and I knew that
the right step had been taken: a film which critically dealt with the
police and apartheid was, at last, available for the public to be seen.
And no cuts were ordered. South Africa could, at last, also demonstrate that its apartheid policy and what flowed from it, was there to

be criticised and be seen by all – its own independent Publications Appeal Board having permitted it to be screened without cuts. This was truly freedom of speech.

However, unbeknown to me, all was not well on the streets. And blood was not flowing as a result of an uprising by black people. "The police are seizing the 35 copies of *Cry Freedom!* in the cinemas!" a *Beeld* journalist exclaimed on the phone. The Board was an independent judicial body and the Commissioner of Police was ignoring our order that the film could be released without cuts. "This could not be true!" I answered. What had become of the Rule of Law? And yet it turned out to be true. I felt numb and exhausted. Persons (obviously right-wing) were calling my staff and telling them that they would "fuck them up" and kill them. The Registrar was in tears. My wife received calls telling her that we would all be killed that very night.

On the six o'clock television news the Minister of Communications, Stoffel van der Merwe, was attempting to explain why the Emergency Regulations could override our decision. A view which was not justifiable in law. Shock. I switched off the television in utter devastation. Police guarded our house for weeks. Shouts from anonymous callers on the phone: "Fuck you! We'll kill you and your family … and burn your house!" The voices came from, we later established, right-wing elements. Whether it was the secret Third Force, I will never know. Shortly afterwards, a Commission of Inquiry found that there was insufficient evidence that such a Third Force existed. The Truth and Reconciliation Commission, after democracy in 1994, reached a different conclusion and the applications before the Amnesty Committee of the Commission confirmed that conclusion.

The South African media gave us its full support in not having banned *Cry Freedom!** There was also wide support from the parliamentary opposition and, of course, anti-apartheid groups in South Africa and abroad.

Three months later, on 3 October 1988, our house was smouldering. The front door had been set alight during the night and the sparks had fallen on a straw hat of my wife. The hat was lying on a nineteenth-century yellowwood table. A hole had burnt through the table top and parts of the carpet were turned into ashes in several places. It was as if someone had shot a flame into the house from under the front door. Could it have been a flame-thrower ("Flammenwerfer"), which had its origins in World War I? The detectives could not establish what the instrument had been. Fortunately, the fire had not spread. My wife was shocked, my children stunned and in tears and the result was a police squad being set up to protect us. The intention had clearly not been to destroy the house, but to harass me. One of the telephone threats in July was indeed that our house would be destroyed. Within a day this was front-page news in all the major newspapers. It was interesting how reporters gained access to our premises by merely showing the police a card. Cameras were flashing as if our house had become public property. Ironically, this was probably also freedom of the press!

Christof Heyns, until recently Dean of the Faculty of Law at the University of Pretoria and an internationally renowned human rights lawyer, who was an assistant of mine early in the 1980s, was permit-

---

*   See, for example, Rina Minervini, "Dignified Van Rooyen just keeps on deciding for himself", *Saturday Star*, 6 August 1988; Rina Minervini, "At times it's hell being a censor in SA – just ask Kobus", *Sunday Star*, 31 July 1988.

ted to pass the police barrier – bringing me a copy of the then recently published Gorbachev's *Perestroika* with an inscription by him honouring my stance.* Another friend, Tony Loubser, brought me a bottle of red wine to soothe a friend who, in his view, must have been about to be fired. An ex-doctoral student, Johann van der Westhuizen, visited me and told me that my participation in the struggle had just started. My answer was that for me the decision was not part of the struggle, but simply resulted from my duty to be independent and rational. Jaco Marais, another ex-student, came to visit me and told me that he admired my independence, although he did not agree with my approach to-media freedom. The *Sunday Times* and other newspapers also sided with us.

A police colonel investigating the arson, ironically, asked me whether the newspaper coverage was true that I had said that the fire had started at 06:00 – for if that were true, I had set the house alight *myself*. Arsonists only operate in the midst of night … Of course I had merely told the press that we had discovered the smouldering front door early in the morning. I was clearly not a hero of the police, which had been vehemently attacked in *Cry Freedom!*

A trained police dog, the German Shepherd Elsa was donated to us for protection. A colonel, who had left South Africa for England for some or other reason, was quoted in *Vrye Weekblad* a year later as having said from London that at the time an unnamed general had told him: "Give the fool a dog that will kill him!"

---

*   I quote the passage (translated from Afrikaans) for the record: "Dear Kobus. With admiration. The values which you strive for – humanity, tolerance, civilisation – are, like wisdom, irrepressible in South Africa and the rest of the world. The fact that, under the most difficult circumstances, you upheld these values, does not only confirm these values, but also stands to your highest credit."

At that time it had been suggested that right-wing elements had probably played a role in the burning of our home. Yes, the film had shown the police to be foolish and brutal in the handling and death of Steve Biko. Yes, viewers were shouting "Amandla!" while watching the film after the state of emergency had been lifted by F.W. de Klerk in 1990. Yes, a black witness for the State's case before us had exclaimed that there would be blood on the streets if the film were to be released. And no, there was never any blood on the streets or violence in theatres and many black viewers were seen to be weeping when leaving the theatres …

Amnesty was later granted by the Truth and Reconciliation Commission to persons who admitted that they had been involved in planting small bombs in theatres when the film was released in 1988. The few slight explosions provided an excuse for the confiscation of the film, in some instances even while the film was being screened. A high-ranking security officer told me the next morning: "This film will never be shown in South Africa." An unbelievable opinion!

Elsa turned out to be a highly intelligent, very caring dog and she became a very close member of the family. For us, her name remains synonymous with security and love. We have keen memories of how she cared for us after disaster had struck. We wept when she died in 1998.

We never learnt who wrote a letter to the *Sowetan* of 6 October 1988 under my name and on Appeal Board official paper, in which I hit out at the government for having seized the film. Cabinet considered firing me (which they were not authorised to do, in any case) as a result of the letter. Ironically, an assistant working for the Cabinet phoned me to ask me whether they could fire me. I simply said "No" and he accepted my answer. This scene could very well have been part of the hilarious, long-running BBC series *The Men from the Ministry!* *

The letter was a magnificent piece of forgery. I could not detect any difference between my signature and the signature on the letter to the *Sowetan*. Experts demonstrated at least twelve points of difference between my handwriting and "my" signature on the letter to the *Sowetan*. Former students of mine sent me telegrammes (it was before e-mail!) congratulating me with the stance I was taking

---

* This light touch parody of the British Civil Service was broadcast by the BBC from 1962 to 1977 and gained worldwide popularity. On the face of it the officials would seem competent, but behind the scenes they are revealed as selfish and incompetent, although friendly, warm and likeable.

in the *Sowetan*. I wish that I had actually written the letter. Paragraphs in the letter read as follows:

> The arbitrary action (the attachment of the copies of the film by the police) was in flagrant disregard of the autonomy of the Publications Appeal Board and the expert evidence collected and opinions formulated by the Board. In over-ruling the carefully considered opinions and decisions of the Board, the Minister and the South African Police have undermined the credibility and authority of the Board ... The banning and the authoritarian actions of the South African Police merely confirm the central message of the film, namely that excessive police action and the arbitrary abuse of power is rife in South Africa and threatens the very fabric of our society. The Publications Appeal Board abhors this abuse of power and disassociates itself from the entire issue.

A retired brigadier in the Security Police and colleague on the Appeal Board, Brigadier Du Preez, told me later that in his time he had written many such letters. I should not be concerned, he said, it would not happen again ... It did not happen again. Did he have inside information? One forgery was, however, sufficient. The State had only tottered slightly as a result of *Cry Freedom!*

Another strange, but most definitely harrowing, experience took place a few days after the arson attack on our house. A man arrived with a rather old truck. He said that he had been phoned by someone who asked him to remove our lounge furniture to a storage centre. He had obtained permission from the police guarding our house to enter our garden. My wife referred him to me. When I saw the man, who suddenly appeared behind me in our garden, I could feel cold fear running down my spine when he told me that he had come to load our lounge furniture. I explained to him that we were being harassed and that his call had obviously been intended to harass us further. I felt sorry for him. Judged by the state of his dilapidated truck, he was obviously not well-off. He reacted by saying that he had been suspicious of the call himself. He had travelled 20 kilometres from his smallholding to our house. He was obviously an innocent pawn in the process, but I suddenly realised how easily someone could enter our premises and, well, kill us.

A further harassing gimmick was an advertisement in *Beeld* which placed our home in the market for a third of its value. Agents flocked to our house because the street number was given in the advertisement. In a moment of ingenuity, I changed our street number by switching a 6 with a 7. For a few days I could see cars passing by our house with agents who were obviously confused by the street numbering. I received an invoice for R29 from *Beeld* for placing the advertisement.

At the time we received a number of phone calls in which we were told that it would not be long before we were killed and that I should resign my post as chairman. I had our phone number changed within two days after the first calls. The calls were all from persons with a typical South African English or Afrikaans-English accent. I never had the impression that the calls had come from Steve Biko supporters. In fact, Steve Biko supporters were said to have had no problems with the film, except that it had given undue prominence to Donald Woods, the editor friend of Steve Biko, who had fled the country earlier.

In retrospect it is clear that the conduct described above was unbridled harassment and nothing more. At the time, of course, we were shocked and feared what could happen. At a certain point we had seven police guards patrolling our premises after we received a call that our house would finally be destroyed that week.

My colleague, Lynda Gilfillan, resigned in protest against what she regarded as a return to stricter rules in a number of cases, and also because of the government's actions in rejecting the *Cry Freedom!* judgment: it had confiscated copies of the film, ignoring our approval of the uncut film. Her minority report against the cuts that were made to the Anant Singh film, *The Stick*, represented her view. I respected her decision to resign.

The decision about *Cry Freedom!* set a new freedom-oriented approach and, looking back, I am astounded that we had the conviction to pass it, given the state of emergency that was still in force. Nevertheless, in 1988 I had reached a stage where the inhuman and cruel strictures of the apartheid regime simply *had* to be published in South Africa. And *Cry Freedom!* was the first effective medium to do so. It could not pose a risk to security. But it did pose a serious risk to the future of apartheid – thank God!

ELEVEN

The end of an era
February – April 1990

WHEN THE END OF MY TERM was announced, members of the media were kind enough to give recognition to my quest for liberty and the results achieved.* I received letters of commendation from many prominent media leaders and authors. Amongst them Doug Band from the Argus Group, John Allen from the International Book Distributors Association, Ton Vosloo from Nasionale Pers and also a concerned phone call from the chairman of the Afrikaans Writers' Guild, Abraham de Vries. Conservative voices must have been overjoyed at my departure. Today, twenty-one years later, I am inclined to smile when thinking about their fervour. Although they demanded my head they could, fortunately, not appropriate my soul …

On my last day at the Publications Appeal Board, we handed down several judgments in a full session of the Appeal Board, unbanning amongst other things Nelson Mandela's *The Struggle is my Life*. The book had been banned quite a while before that. An appeal was lodged in 1989 and we unbanned the book. There was, however, a request from Nelson Mandela that we should not publish our judgment before he was free.

★   See, *inter alia*, Phillip Altbeker, "A man of enlightenment", *Business Day*, 12 April 1990.

I returned to my full-time position as professor at the University of Pretoria – which had seconded me part time to the State for ten years – and had to face a life that seemed dreary compared to the active life which I had led nationally and, at times, internationally. Yet, I was back teaching full time and acting as promoter for doctoral students, which I had chosen as a career when I was 23 years old and which remained a most inspiring task at age 47.

Since the security work had fallen away after 2 February 1990 and a new era had dawned in terms of publications such as *Scope*, *Penthouse* and *Hustler* after 1992, there was not, in any case, that much work and challenges for the Board left. The work which we planned to do – unbanning all literary works of merit and setting a new freedom policy for the works of the disenfranchised majority – was done.

The challenges which had faced us in the eighties were enormous. In the moral field films had changed completely in style as from 1970. For quite a time, one could say since the late fourties, there had been a few compromising kissing scenes in films directed at the ordinary cinemas. The famous beach kissing scene between Burt Lancaster and Deborah Kerr in *From Here to Eternity* (1953) was probably the climax before 1970. Today one can google the forty-second live performance … And, of course, there were the great Alfred Hitchcock thrillers which had a slight nightmare potential to them – I need only mention masterpieces such as *Psycho* (1960), *The Birds* (1963) and *Marnie* (1964).

However, in the seventies and eighties there was a dramatic move to realism: crude and profane language, nudity, sex and explicit violence made their entry into the run-of-the-mill theatre market. The rape scenes in *A Clockwork Orange,* the explicit sex scenes and nudity in *Last Tango in Paris* had no precedent. Although the sixties saw great Bible films, controversial aspects were never included. It was *Jesus Christ Superstar* in the seventies and *The Last Temptation of Christ* at the end of the eighties which confronted audiences with the unconventional: in the first film it was the rock medium and the second the momentary longing of Jesus to get married, as ordinary men would do, which made the films controversial. Add to that the *Satanic Verses* by Salman Rushdie which appeared in the late eighties and the scene has changed completely from conservative propriety to confronting audiences with dramatically justified moral and religious challenges. And yes, of course, especially after 1955, there was the rising voice of the disenfranchised majority with their leaders in security prisons demanding equality and the right to vote.

We could, accordingly, either cut films to pieces or approach them in an entirely new manner. We chose the latter course and with fitting age restrictions and even limitations to art theatres we could open up films for adults to see. In 1996 the Task Group advised Parliament to move non-violent pornography from the backstreets to licensed adult video shops, so that it could be available under the supervision of the Films and Publications Board. In the security field we moved towards freedom, with the pinnacle of our work in the release, without cuts, of *Cry Freedom!*

After thirty years of involvement in film and publication control, I have often been asked whether one does not become so accustomed to the materials that one can no longer see the wood before the trees; or to put it bluntly, whether one does not become depraved and corrupt. It would probably be impossible to give an objective answer. However, any such question attests to a prior, unjustified assumption that human sexuality is evil. What I can say is that certain extremely violent scenes from films do recur in my nightmares, and sometimes even during my waking hours. Amongst these is a scene from Bertolucci's film *1900*, where a farm manager kills a cat in a mad frenzy by banging its head repeatedly against a wall; the hanging scenes in *Apocalypse Now*; the shots of the bodies of disintegrating children during the Vietnam War in *Born on the Fourth of July*; blood dripping from the ceiling onto people having sex in *Angel Heart*; members of the South African Police hitting school children with sjamboks in *Cry Freedom!*

Looking back now, I am pleased that we confronted the problematic materials by way of age restrictions and, later on, classification of films. The right of an adult to choose freely became dominant and rightly so. Freedom of choice is a central value within a constitutional democracy. We already did substantial spadework for this in the eighties and the spadework became law in 1996. In fact, the only job left for me to do on leaving office in 1990 was to ensure that what we had learnt in the eighties would become law. I deal with this in the next chapter.

My leaving the office led to an offer from the Press Council in September 1990 to become the chairman for the next seven years. The broadcasters also asked me to set up the Broadcasting Complaints Commission of South Africa in 1993. I am privileged to still be the chairman at the time of writing this book. I could therefore continue with my work towards media freedom, albeit in two different spheres of the media.

TWELVE
Drafting for freedom
1994–1996

MY SPIRITS WERE LIFTED CONSIDERABLY when Dr Buthelezi, the Minister of Home Affairs under the new Democratic State, in 1994 approached me to chair a Task Group to advise him as to whether the Publications Act of 1974 was unconstitutional and, if so, to draft a new Act. I was back in my old chambers at the Appeal Board and could feel the excitement of transformation and being part of it again. To be honest, I felt vindicated by this appointment by the new government – the apartheid government having not appointed me for a third term as chairman of the Publications Appeal Board in 1990.

The Publications Act of 1974 was clearly not compatible with the new constitution and now the opportunity was there to head a Task Group in writing the first Act of Parliament which directly dealt with fundamental rights under a new dispensation. My colleagues on the Task Group were experts in their respective fields and as representative as a group of ten could be.

It was decided to obtain the latest information from other countries as to what was appropriate within this field. Fortunately Prof. Coetzee, the Director of Publications, and I had built contacts with several countries' film classifiers and we could obtain the latest information from them – notably from Australia, New Zealand, the

UK, Ireland, Germany, the Netherlands, Norway, Sweden, Hong Kong, Singapore and Zimbabwe. Members of the Task Group also visited Egypt, India, Canada and the USA. The Department of Foreign Affairs assisted us in obtaining information on how religious feelings were accommodated in the classification systems of a further twenty countries. We also studied judgments of the US, Canadian, British, Indian and German courts as well as that of the European Court of Human Rights in Strasbourg, France. At that stage our own Constitutional Court had not yet had the opportunity to hear many cases and we could, accordingly, not depend on that source.*

The matter was urgent since we were only granted three months to complete a report and draft a Bill. I was privileged to have had meetings in India with two former Chief Justices. Their sense for justice inspired me towards clarity in legislation which was often obfuscated by terms such as "indecency" and "obscenity". I also have keen memories of working on the draft of the Bill during a weekend at Banff in the Canadian Rockies. My wife would at dawn still be solidly asleep when I would already be struggling with concepts such as "child pornography" in the draft.

A few days later we met with Judge John Sopinka[†] at the Supreme Court in Ottawa – a warm and very experienced lawyer, who assisted us in addressing practical difficulties in drafting legislation. In Buffalo, close to the Niagara falls, the renowned first-amend-

---

*   Particularly informative judgments were to follow in the next two years and I could convey their outcome to Deputy Minister Sisulu, when she addressed Parliament on the new Act in 1996.

†   Renowned for his judgment on pornography and the degradation of women in *R v Butler* in the Canadian Supreme Court.

ment lawyer, Floyd Abrams, brilliantly advised that we should free the arts completely – an idea which we introduced in the draft and which was accepted by Parliament, except in the case of child pornography. However, the Constitutional Court has rightly held in 2003 that even in such a case the art exemption would apply.

The Task Group had no doubt that the Publications Act of 1974 had become constitutionally incompatible on 27 April 1994 when the Interim Constitution became operational. The Task Group handed a 90-page-report to Dr Buthelezi on 3 December 1994 and this report was published by the Government Printers on 3 March 1995.* The report included a draft Bill. The report was described by Judge John Sopinka in a prestige lecture at the University of Pretoria as the best that he had read in this field. Tested against the rights of equality, human dignity, privacy, freedom of religion and conscience, freedom of expression, access to the courts, fair administrative justice, the report stated as follows:

We have reached the conclusion that a new Publications Act is necessary. The present Act intrudes upon the freedom of choice of adults in an unreasonable manner by making bans widely possible; employs

---

*   Its report was published by the Government Printers on 3 March 1995. Members of the Task Group were Prof. Kobus van Rooyen SC (Chairman), Prof. Braam Coetzee, Prof. A.C. Nkabinde, Dr Brigalia Bam, Ms Fawzia Peer, Ms Lauren Jacobson, Adv. Willie Huma, Mr Piet Westra, Prof. Dan Morkel and Adv. Gilbert Marcus SC. The secretariat consisted of the highly competent Mr A. Tredoux and Mr T. O'Neil. The driving force behind the inquiry was Dr Buthelezi and his incomparable team: the Deputy Minister (now Minsiter of Defence) Dr Lindiwe Sisulu, the Director General Mr Piet Colyn and the Deputy Director General, Mr Ivan Lambinon. A copy of the report can be found on www.bccsa.co.za under Annual Reviews.

vague terminology ("offensive, indecent, obscene, harmful to morals"); generally regulates the private domain of an adult too strenu-
ously; gives preference to the Christian religion, which is in conflict
with the equal protection clause; provides for political intervention
by the minister in certain instances; and does not place sufficient emphasis on the freedoms of artistic expression and of scientific research
which are guaranteed by the Constitution.

The ideal was to employ language which would be as clear as possible. Two approaches were combined: as far as possible the factual
circumstances were explained on which a decision would be based
by the Board or, on appeal, by the Review Board.

By exempting art, drama, the products of scientific research and
documentaries from the Act we would ensure that such works would
not, once again, be banned and have to be unbanned by a progres-
sive Appeal Board as in the past: the spectre of the pre-1980 banning of *Magersfontein, Looking on Darkness, Donderdag of Woensdag,
Lady Chatterley's Lover,* Sipho Sepamla's *A Ride on the Whirlwind* and
pre-1980 movies such as *Last Tango in Paris, A Clockwork Orange* and
Jesus Christ Superstar and, of course, many more, demanded freedom
of choice for adults. Of course, these works were already set free in
the 1980s during my tenure as Appeal Board chairman.

There would be no pre-censorship on publications. In the case
of films the distributors agreed to pre-classification for practical
reasons. The words "judged within context" were dominant in the
definition section. The isolated-passage approach would amount
to an irregular form of consideration of a publication or film. It
took many hours to convince the Portfolio Committee to add these
words even in the case of child pornography. Only hard pornogra-

phy (XX) would be prohibited for distribution and, in that category, only child pornography would be prohibited for possession. Child pornography was the only material that was also subjected to an automatic ban on importation, production and possession. Other forms of XX and X18 material could be possessed and even be imported. The embarrassment which, in darker apartheid years, faced travellers returning from overseas at our international airports, would no longer exist!

Hard pornography (XX) would be visual images of child pornography, explicit violence mixed with explicit sex, bestiality, gender-degrading sex and certain forms of extreme violence. X18 would be films and publications predominantly containing visual images or descriptions of explicit sexual conduct between consenting adults – "sexual conduct" amounting to particularly intimate sexual acts – were listed in the Act. Of course, if these elements were justified by drama, scientific research or art, they would not be classified in any of the two categories and be subjected only to an age restriction and classification; the latter informing viewers of the possible risqué content of the film.

However, art could not save child pornography. The Home Affairs Portfolio Committee was not prepared to exempt art which depicted what was defined as prohibited child sex or nudity at the time. In all other respects the report was accepted by the Portfolio Committee. As mentioned earlier, the Constitutional Court has, commendably, held in 2003 that the art exemption was applicable in this case as well and that works of art would not be subject to a ban.[*]

But how did the conservative community react to the news that

---

[*]   *De Reuck v Director of Public Prosecutions and Others* 2004(1) SA 406(CC).

pornography would be available at licensed shops? We held hearings in Johannesburg, Cape Town, Pretoria and Durban. More than 1500 representations were received. The anti-pornography lobby was up in arms. A *Sunday Times* front-page headline proclaimed confidently that pornography would now be available. Dr Gerrit Viljoen, an ex-Broederbond leader and Minister in the last apartheid cabinet, who was otherwise in favour of the new democracy, declared at a public debate with me, that the legalisation of pornography posed a grave risk. I replied that pornography had been available on the black market for many years and that making it available to adults in licensed video shops would normalise the matter. The conservative audience was not impressed.

ONCE AGAIN, I WAS BRANDED AS AN utter fool in conservative circles. "He is selling us out!" a group chanted when I was about to speak at a dinner. When I took the podium I was simply boo-ed off by the same group. Real barbarians, I thought. At a function an ex-student, whom I attempted to greet, gave me a cold shoulder and simply said: "We are not supposed to be on speaking terms! You have forsaken the Afrikaner Christian!"

At one of our public hearings a woman jumped on a table around which committee members were sitting and shouted: "God will send you all to utter damnation! The devil is in you!" She calmed down – and was obviously surprised – when I thanked her for her contribution and offered to pay her travel costs.

WHEN THE REPORT AND DRAFT BILL were taken to Cabinet, the National Party objected and the matter had to be passed over to a second meeting of the Cabinet. The Party also objected to the possibility that non-violent pornography could be rented by persons over the age of 18 years in licensed video shops. I was utterly disappointed.

Although a few questions were still asked by National Party members, the Bill was supported at the second meeting of Cabinet. Deputy President De Klerk chaired the meeting initially. President Mandela entered the room while I was summarising the proposal to the Cabinet. When I left, it was a special moment for me when the President stood up and warmly greeted me at the door. We had met each other in Kyoto in 1991 where he opened an international congress of the International Press Institute. When I left, I heard him say: "Wish we were back in Kyoto!" What a remarkable memory. What a unique man.

The Bill was put forward by Deputy Minister (now Minister) Dr Lindiwe Sisulu and accepted by Parliament unanimously. Almost no amendments had been made to the draft Bill put forward by the Task Group.

IT DOES NOT FALL WITHIN THE AMBIT of this book to analyse in detail the amendments to the Act in 1999, 2004 and in 2009. However, the Act runs a real risk of constitutional challenge insofar as the amendments returned to vague language in the definition section and insofar as pre-classification of some publications has been introduced.

Although the basic principles protecting drama, the products of science and art are still included in the Act, it is profoundly sad for me to see how the Act has been amended in the past eleven years. The Act, which was a product of the freedom-seeking 1994 government, has now been stacked with all kinds of limiting provisions. The worst ones are probably a duty to pre-clear certain materials, the extension of the Act to South Africans who are in a foreign country, the inclusion of the written word when it applies to child pornography and the ban on the possession of such works even if they are justified by art, products of science, drama and documentaries. These provisions are clearly unconstitutional. I am, however, not arguing that the production of films and photographs featuring or showing children should ever be placed beyond the reach of the law. Children under 18 should and are still protected against taking part in sex scenes in films. The ban extends to exploitation of nudity as well. These instances are defined with particularity in the legislation and also in codes that govern the press and broadcasters.

I will deal with child pornography and art more fully in the next chapter and in Addendum Three.

THIRTEEN
Child pornography and art
1998–2009

THE NEW FILMS AND PUBLICATIONS ACT had hardly been put into operation in 1998 when the Grahamstown Arts Festival tested the new Board and controversy followed. The *Viscera* exhibition by Mark Hipper at the Festival was held by the Board and Review Board to have not amounted to child pornography when judged in context. The exhibition – restricted to adults – illustrated the perversity of child sexual abuse. The Deputy Minister of Home Affairs disagreed and her view was reported in the media. The Deputy Minister, in obvious reaction to the Board's decision, appointed a Task Team. The Task Team advised that the original section 27, which prohibits by way of criminal sanction the possession of child pornography, was not comprehensive enough to counter child pornography. Since the original section required that context must be taken into consideration when judging whether a visual presentation in films and publications amounts to child pornography, the Task Team argued that the reference to context provided a "loophole" for child pornographers, as happened at the *Viscera* exhibition.

Accordingly, the original definition was repealed by Parliament and substituted by what may only be regarded as a too wide* and

---

*   In other words it included areas that were not in need of regulation by law, e.g. art and scientific publications.

vague definition, which could merely be remedied by a substantial limiting interpretation by the Constitutional Court. By excluding context, the aim was clearly to negate the Review Board judgment on the *Viscera* exhibition, the Review Board having accentuated context in its judgment, which held the photographs not to have contravened the definition in the Act. The Task Team rejected the contextual approach in the Act of 1996 which I had argued for and which was accepted by Parliament.

The matter fortunately came before the Constitutional Court in the 2003 *De Reuck* matter.

FOR PURPOSES OF THE PRODUCTION OF A television documentary, Tascoe De Reuck, who had been a part-time television presenter and a film producer (acclaimed as a student at the Pretoria Technikon) began to investigate in 1999 the illegitimate availability of child pornography on the internet. He collected a large number of examples printed out from internet websites and which he, at times, had to access after having had to (falsely) "prove"* to underground website managers that he had a sexual interest in child pornography. The police were alerted to his activities by an informer and obtained a search warrant from a magistrate in terms of section 27(3) of the Films and Publications Act of 1996, after the permission of the Director of Public Prosecutions, Witwatersrand, had been obtained. He and his landlord were both arrested and had to spend a night in police cells. The arrest was widely publicised, especially since his landlord was (and still is) a famous and respected

---

*   This was the only way in which he could gain access.

film critic and writer. After a few months the charges against the landlord were rightly withdrawn on the basis that he had been unaware that De Reuck was involved in this project and was in possession of a wide variety of photographs.

De Reuck was charged in the Randburg Regional Court with the possession of these photographs. The matter was postponed so that he could test the constitutionality of section 27 of the Films and Publications Act, as amended in 1999.

The argument before the High Court as well as the Constitutional Court was that the new section 27 was too broad since it unreasonably interfered with the right to artistic and scientific creativity; the latter including the right to possess child pornography where a researcher – who would include a film producer – had such materials in his or her possession for purposes of research. De Reuck's integrity as a bona fide film producer was never in dispute. The question was whether the Act permitted him to argue in a prosecution that the material was held with the intention to produce the said documentary. The Constitutional Court held that this was not a defence and that he should have obtained permission from the Executive of the Film and Publications Board in terms of section 22 of the Act. In the United States, Canada, Ireland, the United Kingdom, Germany and New Zealand this is a legal defence without prior permission from the authorities.

The Constitutional Court declined to invalidate the definition. However, it limited the wide definition of child pornography to what was not that much different from the definition originally drafted by the Task Group and accepted by Parliament in 1996. The Court, nonetheless, added the word "explicit" and added that where the work – judged as a whole and in context – gave rise to aesthetical as opposed to sexual appeal, the photographs et cetera would not amount to child pornography. With this the Court went further than Parliament which explicitly excluded art as a defence in the case of child pornography.

When after the constitutional hearings De Reuck nevertheless had to stand trial, the Regional Court also did not question the fact that he was a bona fide film producer and that he had possessed the materials for purposes of research to produce a documentary. However, since the Constitutional Court had held that section 27 did not permit such a defence, he could only refer to his research purpose in mitigation. The Regional Court took this into consideration when it imposed its sentence of one year imprisonment or a R24 000 fine, half of which was suspended. De Reuck immediately paid the fine.

A particularly negative article against De Reuck then appeared in the newspaper *Beeld*. The article questioned why he was now pleading guilty and suggested that possessors of child pornography were paedophiles. *Beeld* was taken to the Press Ombudsman by his attorney, Barry Sim. The Ombudsman ruled that *Beeld* had to apologise to De Reuck that their article incorrectly implied that he was a paedophile and that he had belatedly altered his defence from that of having been a bona fide film producer to guilty.

What *Beeld* apparently did not understand was that the Constitutional Court had held that the Films and Publications Act did not permit De Reuck to defend himself on the merits with reference to his profession and accordingly he had to plead guilty. His professional plea was a mitigating circumstance. In a sense the Ombudsman's ruling was a moral victory for De Reuck and his legal team.

Further comments on the judgment of the Constitutional Court are to be found in Addendum Three of this book.

FOURTEEN

Freedom!
1994–2011

WHAT FOLLOWS IS BACKGROUND and a personal synopsis of what the task of the State is in regulating films and publications as to content. The views relate specifically to statutory control. I am a firm believer in effective and independent controls set up by the media itself. However, the intention of this book is to discuss state control of films and publications. Excluded would, accordingly, be newspapers that fall under the Press Ombudsman and broadcasts that fall under the Broadcasting Complaints Commission of South Africa.*

In our work as members of the Publications Appeal Board we did not judge pornography as such. Only films due for public screening came before us. And since distributors knew that pornography would not be permitted, such cases were not even brought before the publications committees. On the other hand, the criminal courts were tasked with evaluating pornography in terms of the Indecent or Obscene Photographic Matter Act of 1967. This Act was declared to be constitutionally invalid in 1996.

Here are some general thoughts on censorship:

---

*   Only broadcasters who consent to the BCCSA jurisdiction and are members of the National Association of Broadcasters or the Christian Association of Broadcasters fall under its jurisdiction. In practice this amounts to all commercial broadcasters and some community broadcasters.

First, I have never believed that any kind of material – whether a book or a film – can deprave or corrupt an adult reader or viewer. Of course, where a person is mentally challenged, violent or sexual film or video material might well provide a link to antisocial conduct. But that might be true of any kind of object – from sweets to shoes to nude female breasts – as pointed out by Justice Kennedy of the US Supreme Court in *Ashcroft.** And, of course, to apply that test would place all drama, literature, science, documentaries and films at risk: the disturbed mind rather than the "reasonable" mind would become the test.

Second, all material must be judged in context. Therefore, any approach where parts of a novel, play or film are quoted out of context so as to demonstrate its harmfulness, is rejected. The isolated-passage approach to censorship is rightly anathema to literary experts and legal scholars. The approach was probably applied by the Appellate Division in its finding of undesirability in the case of Wilbur Smith's *When the Lion Feeds,* in terms of the Act of 1963 in 1965. However, Chief Justice Ogilvie Thompson rejected this isolated-passage approach early in the seventies and my directions to the Appeal Board in the eighties were that context was all-important in judging a work. When in 1994 we drafted the new Films and Publications Act of 1996, we ensured that the words "judged in context" ran through the Act like a golden thread. Past experience of quotes out of context to condemn a novel, ensured that context was a paramount consideration. After Parliament attempted to exclude context in a 1999 amendment of the "child pornography"

---

*   *Ashcroft v Free Speech Coalition et al.* 122 S.Ct.1389 (16 April 2002) at p. 10–11.

definition, the Constitutional Court in 2003 rejected any approach according to which context would not be relevant. The 1994 Task Group was vindicated by this judgment: context would be relevant in all cases, even in the case of alleged child pornography.

Third, the intolerance of fundamentalists must be ignored. It is frightening how some politicians have at times bent over backwards to please the moral and religious claims of fundamentalists – which was especially true of apartheid South Africa. Many voters love the sound of "No, that is enough!" I experienced this with the ban on *Magersfontein, O Magersfontein!* in 1977. When I told Dr Schlebusch, the new Minister of Home Affairs, in 1980 that we had lifted the ban on *Magersfontein* and that he might wish to mention this in his next party political speech – which happened to take place at a small town, Fauresmith, not too distant from where the Boer War struggle of *Magersfontein* had taken place – he smiled and said that that would be a mistake: voters were generally conservative and would not regard the lifting of the ban of a book in which the name of the Lord was used in vain as "good news". Of course, judged in context, the profanity could be explained as an essential part of that brilliant satire.

Fourth, threats of violence if a finding is made in favour of a film that may be problematic as a result of religious or other reasons, are irrelevant in an adjudication. Of course, if the material itself advocates violence based on religion, that would place it in the category of hate speech. When a Court* interdicted newspapers from publishing cartoons of the Prophet Mohammed, it based the interdict

---

*   *See Jamiat-Ul-Ulama of Transvaal v Johncom Media Investment Ltd and Others* WLD case 1127/06.

on the protection of the dignity of Muslims regarding their religious adherence to the teachings of the Prophet. There was, rightly, no reference to threats of possible violence in the conclusion reached by the Court, in spite of this aspect having been raised by the applicant in its papers before the Court.

Fifth, it is true that Parliament represents the electorate and that the Constitutional Court has held that Parliament has the right to protect morality. But then the Constitutional Court defines morality as constitutional morality.* That clearly means that Parliament may not simply give in to the voice of moral fundamentalists or even to the voice of the majority. The Court also, rightly, rejected religious doctrine as a source for the interpretation of the Constitution and emphasised freedom of choice.†

Sixth, greater language clarity in legislation and adjudication regarding the criteria to be applied must be a constant legislative aim. Terminology used in legislation such as "offensive", "indecent", "obscene" and "harmful to public morals", which was to be found in the Publications Act of 1974 and its predecessor, as well as in the Indecent or Obscene Photographic Matter Act of 1967, has been regarded as too vague to withstand constitutional scrutiny. When drafting the Films and Publication Act in 1994, the Task Group already expressed criticism against this kind of language. Consequently, the said terms were not included in the new legislation. Two years later the Constitutional Court applied the same approach

---

*   *S v Jordan and Others (Sex Workers Education & Advocacy Task Force & Others as Amici Curiae)* 2002(6) SA 642(CC).

†   *Minister of Home Affairs v Fourie (Doctors for Life International and Others, Amici Curiae); Lesbian and Gay Equality Project and Others v Minister of Home Affairs* 2006(1) SA 524(CC).

when it effectively held the Indecent or Obscene Photographic Matter Act of 1967 to be invalid as a result of the vagueness of the terms "indecent" and "obscene".*

Seventh, an adult must have the right to choose when material has not, judged in context, clearly been shown to fall under the categories mentioned below. That is why the 1994 Task Group introduced the concept of licensed porn shops. Only a limited category of materials, including the following, is forbidden for distribution: child pornography, violent sex, bestiality, material that advocates hatred based on gender, religion, race, ethnicity and excessive violence. However, apart from child pornography, the materials could be possessed and imported. Important to note is that drama, literature, science and art are not included in the ban. It is believed that age restrictions and classification would protect children and sensitive viewers in these cases.

Eighth, the protection of children is important. However, the claim that since section 28(2) of the Constitution provides that a child's best interests are paramount in every matter concerning the child and that, whatever any other fundamental right guarantees, section 28 is conclusive on the matter, is unfounded. Balancing of rights must always take place, even in such a case. The Constitutional Court has held that when a matter is adjudicated in terms of the Bill of Rights, the Court should approach the fundamental rights from the point of view of their being equal, and then balance those rights.†

---

*   *Case and Another v Minister of Safety and Security and Others; Curtis v Minister of Safety and Security and Others* 1996 (3) SA 617 (CC).

†   *De Reuck v Director of Public Prosecutions and Others* 2004(1) SA 406(CC).

An important aspect of Constitutional Court doctrine is that freedom of expression includes the right to express offensive ideas. The limit would be reached when the reasonableness test of section 36 is not satisfied. Nevertheless, the starting point is of particular significance. Under the pre-1996 publications and films legislation, "offensive to public morals" was an important basis for banning. The language in *Lady Chatterley's Lover* and *Magersfontein, O Magersfontein!* was rejected simply on the grounds of it being "offensive" to public morals before 1980. And, of course, one of the criteria for a banning on religious grounds was offensiveness to religious convictions or feelings. Hence, the Appellate Division banned the sound recording of *Jesus Christ Superstar*. The Publications Appeal Board did the same with Martin Scorsese's film *The Last Temptation of Christ*, despite its open-minded approach in other respects. Fortunately, these films have now been cleared for DVD, video and broadcasting. As a result of the fact that the distribution of the film was stopped by its owners in 2000, the film remains effectively banned for theatres, after the theatrical distribution was not permitted by the Films and Publications Board in 1999.

Finally, when one is involved in any form of regulation of the media, one must have respect for films and the printed word. This was impressed upon me by my parents, who were both authors and read extensively. The fact that we lived in rural areas most of our lives, also confronted me with the hardships of rural black people. When the Appeal Board unbanned the 1955 document the *Freedom Charter* in 1984, I had an understanding of the demand for equality and justice which it expressed. When our home was set alight by right-wing elements in 1988 after the Appeal Board had passed *Cry Freedom!*, I knew that I had in some way become part of a struggle for equality and had, at least, done something to further that struggle. My wife and children had also suffered personal trauma as a result of the incident. This trauma was, of course, minor in comparison with the suffering caused to the majority of South Africans by the apartheid system.

TO LIVE IN A CONSTITUTIONAL DEMOCRACY that guarantees freedom of expression is a privilege. To have been closely involved in furthering freedom, in my own way, for more than thirty years, has been an enormous privilege. My love of books and films, and respect for the principle of freedom of expression, eventually came to some kind of fruition in my work. Fortunately, the Constitution has introduced a new paradigm within which books and films must be judged.

Subsequently, when the majority of the first Tribunal at the Broadcasting Complaints Commission voted against the late-night screening by etv of *The Last Temptation of Christ* in 2007, I filed a minority judgment. Although the material would have been offensive to the vast majority of Christians, the 23:15 screening was legitimate in terms of the Broadcasting Code. The film amounted to splendid drama, and adults had the right to choose to see it. The time of screening, the spoken warning, the classification and the 18 age restriction all made it possible for viewers to make an informed decision. On (internal) appeal it was held that the broadcast had indeed been permissible, since Jesus had, once again, rejected the temptation.

The Last Temptation of Christ was my ultimate test as a lawyer and a Christian. I could not simply find that it would be tolerable for

Christians that the film was broadcast at 23:15 with the necessary age restriction and classification. The conclusion had to be based on legal grounds that were not applicable when the Publications Appeal Board held the film to be offensive in 1989. In Addendum Four to this book, more is said about the judging of this film.

It was, ultimately, a liberating experience to breathe the fresh air of freedom of choice.

Epilogue

LOOKING BACK ON A CAREER CLOSELY connected to the control of films, publications and broadcast content – spanning more than three decades – one cannot help to consider what forces may have been at work in changing the views of a rather conservative 32-year-old to those of a freedom devotee. If one compares the stifling wording of the Act of 1974 with the Act of 1996, which was drafted by the Task Group, there is a dramatic move to allow adults the freedom to read and view almost any material. The paradigm shifted from "when in doubt, ban" to "when in doubt, set free". And, of course: "Don't cut!"

The Act of 1996 demonstrated a respect for the arts and introduced a new era, which followed the freedom-oriented approach of 1990, the year I left the Appeal Board. But now, the wording of the Act also spoke of freedom. Ideology would no longer be the basis for a ban. Fortunately, the Appeal Board of the 1980s did not support the apartheid approach, and instead strove for freedom of expression. This principle was enshrined in the new 1996 legislation. Only a real risk of harm, applicable especially to children, could justify a limitation under the new Act. Additional limits placed on hate speech, child pornography and violent sex, are all constitutionally justifiable.

I have attempted to explain the process I had gone through in being shocked into change by what I had come to experience within the censorship machinery. Fortunately, the vagueness in the terminology employed by the Act of 1974 granted the Appeal Board the opportunity to interpret the Act in line with the principle of freedom of expression, which included the right to artistic and dramatic freedom and permitted the call for democracy and equality.

By 1990, three prominent matters still had to be resolved: *The Last Temptation of Christ*, Salman Rushdie's *Satanic Verses*, and the large number of works banned under the security paragraph and which never reached the Appeal Board. The new Films and Publications Board approved the video and DVD versions of *The Last Temptation of Christ*. The Appeal Tribunal of the Broadcasting Complaints Commission, in 2007, held that the broadcast of *The Last Temptation of Christ* was permissible for late-night viewing by adults who might choose to watch it. As for *Satanic Verses*, the new Board increased its availability by arguing that its availability was necessary to ensure that scholars would remain informed.

After the ANC and other organisations were unbanned in 1990, Prof. Coetzee, Director of the Publications Directorate, commenced unbanning all materials, the ban of which had previously been connected to the ban on the ANC and other organisations.

The opportunity granted to me in 1994–1996 by the new democratic government to preside over the Task Group that drafted the new Films and Publications Act of 1996, was a unique one. We were able to create a new landscape for film and publication regulation. I was also privileged in 2009, as Councillor, to chair a committee of the Independent Communications Authority that drafted the most recent Code for broadcasters. The Code accords with constitutional values. As a result – in contrast to the Films and Publications Act as amended in 2009 – dramatic, documentary and artistic merit would be a defence for broadcasters, even in the case of child pornography.

IN 2009 WHEN MY WIFE AND I saw the film *Elegy*, based on a novel of the acclaimed author, Philip Roth, we had a sense of satisfaction about the struggle for the recognition of the merits of drama. Had the film been considered by the Publications Appeal Board in the seventies, the sex scenes and the shots of nude female breasts would certainly have been excised. However, in the late eighties no cuts would have been ordered by the Appeal Board.

We were similarly impressed by the film, *The Reader*, in the same year. As indicated earlier, in the eighties the Appeal Board set out to recognise dramatic merit, and this ground was by now explicitly recognised in the new Films and Publications Act of 1996.

It is unfortunate and in any case not compatible with our Constitution, that art, drama and documentary material are not exempted in terms of the 2009 amendment to the Films and Publications Act in so far as child pornography is concerned. The Legislature has, with respect, seemingly not taken note of the Constitutional Court's judgment in *De Reuck*,[*] where these values are recognised, even in the case of child pornography. Fortunately, the three defences apply in all other cases. However, it is not unlikely that Prof. Govender, the chairperson of the Review Board under the Films and Publications Act, will, as he did in his judgment on *XXY*,[†] nevertheless apply *De Reuck*.

---

[*]   2004(1) SA 406(CC).

[†]   A film of special merit which deals with the problems of a young boy who has both female and male genitals.

A contextual approach also remains obligatory. The defences relating to artistic and dramatic material, as well as a contextual approach, have been hallmarks of what has been striven for over the past thirty years. As long as they remain, there is hope for freedom of artistic and dramatic expression, and the right to be informed.

A PIVOTAL MOMENT IN MY PERSONAL development was probably the orchestrated 1977 campaign against the acclaimed Afrikaans satire *Magersfontein, O Magersfontein!*, which the Appeal Board subsequently banned in 1977. It was known that Etienne Leroux had suffered emotional pain as a result of the banning of his novel by members of his own Afrikaans community. This, together with the shocking prejudice against *Magersfontein, O Magersfontein!*, catapulted me into realising that such bannings should never be repeated. Crude and profane words from the book were quoted out of context in letters accompanying the petitions, which were sent to various organisations and church councils. This was indeed a shame on South Africa.

There was a sense of freedom when, in March 1980, the Appeal Board unbanned *Magersfontein, O Magersfontein!* Having breathed the fresh air of freedom one could only fall in love with it. Yet, the flame of freedom must constantly be kindled to keep it alive.

THE PINNACLE OF DEMOCRATIC FREEDOM with regard to films and publications lay in the unbanning of the *Freedom Charter* in 1984; the unbanning of *New Nation* and *South* in 1987; and, of course, the passing of the Attenborough film, *Cry Freedom!*, in 1988. The mood of distress and shock that arrived a day later when the Commis-

sioner of Police had all the copies of the film confiscated, is inde-
scribable. It made no sense that South Africans should be "protected" against this important film. I recently spoke to Zwelakhe
Sisulu, who was editor of the *New Nation* newspaper in the 1980s.
We shared memories of the disgust generally felt by the three-
month ban by the Minister on his newspaper. Yet, we were also
able to share memories of the more enlightened approach of the
Publications Appeal Board at the time, as it moved away from the
influence of the apartheid state.

In 1990 when *Cry Freedom!* was screened in a public cinema
after the state of emergency had been lifted and Nelson Mandela
had been released, cries of Amandla! could be heard. People were
weeping as they left the cinema. South Africa was truly on its path
to freedom, and it was clear that our trust in audiences was not
misplaced. In spite of warnings that the screening of the film would
lead to the disruption of public order, there was no blood on the
streets. I had prayed for strength and independence on the morning
before the *Cry Freedom!* hearing commenced in 1988, and in 1990
the outcome was visible: there was freedom in the air and on the
streets.

The paradigm had shifted in film and publication regulation: from
no to yes, from distrust to trust, from fundamentalism to realism,
from despotism to democracy.

ADDENDA

Addendum One: Members of the Appeal Board 1975–1990

For the record, the first Appeal Board consisted of Mr Justice J.H. (Lammie) Snyman (chairman), Proff. Kobus van Rooyen (deputy), Alwyn Grové, Anna Neethling-Pohl, Drs Klaas van Wyk de Vries and G. Williams. Both Dr Williams and Dr van Wyk de Vries, sadly, passed away during the first term, which was five years. The former was replaced by Mr Desmond Abernethy, retired principal of Boys High School, Pretoria and the latter by Dr Cassie Venter, who was from the Gereformeerde Church.

In 1977 the following persons were added to the panel after the Act had been amended to provide for twelve members: Gen. Gideon Joubert (retired Commissioner of Police), Rev. Piet van der Merwe from the Dutch Reformed Church, Mr Wilcocks, a retired regional magistrate, Mr Douglas Fuchs, retired Director-General of the SABC, Mr Hans Fourie, retired Secretary of Home Affairs and Rev. F.C. Louw, from the Methodist Church.

In 1980 Proff. Nic Sabbagha and Réna Pretorius joined the Board in the place of Mr Fourie and Mr Wilcocks. Rev. Kotie de Jager replaced Dr Cassie Venter, who had accepted a position in Cape Town. Mr Hugo Malherbe, who was described as the doyen of regional magistrates when he retired, became the Deputy Chairman in 1980. He was a quiet-spoken, well-read person and most certainly lived up to his splendid reputation and supported me fully in the plans to liberalise the controls. Proff. Grové, Neethling-Pohl, Gen. Joubert and Mr Abernethy remained on the Board.

Later in the 1980s the Board was joined by Prof. Pieter Oosthuizen (later to become senior counsel) as Deputy Chair replacing Mr Malherbe, Prof. Mike Hough (a political analyst and security expert) and Brig. Du Preez, who had been a member of the Security Police. Mrs Lynda Gilfillan (now Dr) also joined the Board by 1987, replacing Prof. Sabbagha. Adv. P. Paizes joined the Board in 1989. It should be noted that the terms were, according to the Act, five-year terms.

In 1985 the Board was also joined by Prof. A.L. Mawasha, Rev. J.J. Mettler and Mr A. Ramsamy – the first appointments from the disenfranchised majority. Co-opted members to the Appeal Board were, over the years, Prof. Marthinus Vorster, professor of Public Law at UP, Mr Jan van der Walt, retired high school principal, Mr Justus Tshungu, a broadcaster, Mrs Liliètte Radloff, an ex-teacher, Dr Linda Venter, a lecturer in Communications at the then RAU, Dr Willie Botha from the Dutch Reformed Church central administration, Prof. Fanie van Jaarsveld, a professor in Law at UP, Prof. Gerrit Velthuizen, a professor in Theology at UP, Prof. Dave Beyers, a professor in Psychology at UP, Moulana Jeena from the Transvaal Jamiat-Ul-Ulama, Mrs Penina Goldstein, an ex-teacher, Prof. Yvonne Burns, a professor in Law at Unisa, Mrs Cecile Marais, a senior librarian at Unisa and Mrs Rita Scholtz, wife of the literarian, Prof. Merwe Scholtz.

From 1975 the registrars were Mr Ernst Storm, Mrs Lulu Malan and Mrs Mariana Rautenbach. In 1990 Adv. Louis Pienaar and, later on, Prof. Dan Morkel became chairmen of the Appeal Board. Prof. Coetzee remained the Director of Publications until the new Act became operational in 1998.

Addendum Two: Reasons of Films and Publications Board
regarding new dispensation for Salman Rushdie's *Satanic Verses*

1. Following the lifting of restrictions on Salman Rushdie's *The Satanic Verses* in January 2002, the Board received a large number of complaints from the public, requesting restrictions to be re-imposed on the distribution of this novel. The majority of complaints came from members of the Muslim community. The substance of the complaints was that *The Satanic Verses* is blasphemous, an insult to Islamic integrity and dignity and a denigration of the character of the Prophet Mohammed. Some of the complaints originated from leading Islamic groups, including the Muslim Judicial Council of the Cape, the Islamic Council of South Africa (Transvaal) and the Jamiat-Ul-Ulama and the Council of Muslim Theologians. The complaints were very strongly worded and, in some cases, contained more than a hint at violent

protests if restrictions on the novel were not reinstated. A profound sense of anger, dismay and disappointment at the lifting of restrictions was evident in all the complaints.

2. The Board was sympathetic to the charge of blasphemy and of severe hurt to the religious sensibilities of the Muslim community. While it is incumbent on the Board to be sensitive to the values of every faith system and every cultural community in South Africa, it might be argued that in a secular state, questions of religious propriety have no place in governmental decision-making. But the Constitution makes it clear that religious freedom and dignity are to be protected by the state. And although the Board was dismayed by threats of public violence contained in some of the complaints, it is aware of the international context and history of Muslim opposition to this novel and accepts its responsibility to treat the complaints seriously. The Board regrets that there was no personal representation by any of the complainants or their representatives at the hearing on the novel. It would have been helpful to have heard the views of complainants in person. Even so, the body of correspondence from complainants is unambiguous in its anger and hurt.

3. The written wish of all the complainants was that the restrictions imposed on the distribution of *The Satanic Verses* should not have been removed and that restrictions to prohibit its distribution in South Africa should be reinstated. The list of restricted publications is a legacy from the previous regime and no longer enjoys any legal force under the Constitution. The lifting of restrictions was nothing more than a technicality in correcting the records where the previous decision is inconsistent with the Constitution. There was no intention on the part of the Board to offend Islam, as some complainants have suggested.

4. The Board no longer uses the concept of outright "banning" of material, except with respect to child pornography. The only other instance when the strongest form of restriction may be considered is with respect to Schedule 10 of the Films and Publications Act, 1996. According to Schedule 10, the Board may restrict a publication from all public access by imposing an "XX" classification if it is judged to be a publication which advocates harm based on religion and which constitutes incitement to cause harm. However, if the publication is a bona fide scientific, documentary, artistic, literary or

religious publication, or if it amounts to a bona fide discussion, argument or opinion pertaining to religion, belief or conscience, or to a matter of public interest, then even if the prior consideration (advocacy of harm based on religion and constituting incitement to cause harm) is valid, the publication may not be classified "XX". This being the case, the option would then be to investigate whether "X18" (making the publication available for distribution to adults from within "adult premises") or a lesser age restriction may be imposed.

5. The Board noted that although *The Satanic Verses* is considered profoundly blasphemous and injurious to the Muslim community, it does not in fact advocate hatred against Islam or indeed against any other religion or faith system. The material which is found to be injurious is a parody – a literary deconstruction of ancient Islamic lore and belief, which is an unpacking of tenets of faith by an author who, in the novel, questions the basis of his own belief. Salman Rushdie's Rabelaisian scepticism may well be profoundly shocking and hurtful to many of the Islamic faith, but it does not invite hatred towards Islam. It certainly does not argue, in its pages, any incitement to cause harm or civil violence. *The Satanic Verses* is without argument a bona fide literary work by a leading international literary figure. On these grounds it is not legally possible for the Board to consider an "XX" classification for this novel.

6. However, the Board cannot ignore religious sensibilities and the sense of profound outrage and hurt which the majority of Muslims feel towards this novel. The Board is aware of the fourteen-year history of Islamic opposition towards *The Satanic Verses* and is sympathetic to the representations which were received from distinguished Islamic groups in South Africa, as well as from very many individual members of the Muslim community. On these grounds, the Board has come to a decision to apply an "X18" classification to *The Satanic Verses*.

7. "X18" is not entirely appropriate for this novel in that it merely sets an age restriction of 18 years for public distribution. There is no doubt that this kind of restriction will not satisfy the concerns of the complainants. Therefore, in accordance with section 36 of the Constitution which allows for "limitations to freedom of expression", [we] modify the "X18" restrictions as follows: *The Satanic Verses* is restricted from all forms of commercial public

distribution in retail outlets, except to the libraries of all bona fide universities, technical colleges or other tertiary institutions, and to all South African legal deposit libraries. It should be available at these institutions to any scholars and members of the public of any age, who wish to read it.

8. In this manner students of literature may have access to the novel, and so may members of the public who do not share the objections which are felt by some members of the Muslim community. There can be no restriction of any kind on personal possession, nor any restriction of any kind on personal importation of this novel, whether by the purchaser in person, or by means of international mail-order services, or any other means either of postal delivery, or on the commercial importation of copies for sale or distribution to the institutions referred to above. Given the transnational nature of the contemporary book trade, the Board believes these measures to be reasonable and just.

9. The substance of the decision is that *The Satanic Verses* should not be for sale in public in South African commercial booksellers or any other commercial outlet, nor should it be available for borrowing from any municipal or public library other than the legal deposits referred to above. This will ensure that the novel is limited to circulation only among bona fide students of literature, including Muslim theologians who may wish to substantiate their views on the novelist's portrayal of Islam, and who have the right to read it, while protecting members of the South African Muslim community from further grave offence.

10. The decision given here is an attempt to satisfy the theological and religious concerns of the South African Muslim community while allowing for the crucial principle of right of access and freedom of expression within a controlled context.

Addendum Three: Child pornography and art

The definition of child pornography which came before the Constitutional Court in the *De Reuck* case survived, but only after narrowing of the 1999 amendment to section 27 of the Act. The Constitutional Court ensured that the definition would be in accordance with the freedom to impart and to receive information. The Constitutional Court also defined child pornography in such a manner that the material had to be judged within context; that visual material which, judged as a whole, has as its predominant objective purpose the stimulation of erotic feeling in its target audience, is pornography. Any image which, judged as a whole, predominantly stimulates aesthetic feeling is therefore not caught by the definition. The Constitutional Court then delineated the four categories that are to be found in the definition and included that it must be explicit: the image would not be child pornography unless it explicitly depicts: a child* engaged in sexual conduct; a child engaged in a display of genitals; a child participating in sexual conduct; or a child assisting another person to engage in sexual conduct for the purposes of stimulating sexual arousal in the target audience. The test is the objective one of the reasonable viewer, who would not necessarily be aroused himself or herself. "Sexual conduct" is as defined in the Act.

Since the Court has, in effect, amended the wording of the definition by adding ("explicit") and exempting, it would have been in the interests of justice for Parliament to have replaced the definition in the 2004 and 2009 amending Acts with the definition the Court has, in effect, held to be the constitutionally justifiable definition. It would assist those who are involved in the detection of crime, and those who apply the Act. Persons who seek to possess or import pornography for research, must obtain permission from the Executive of the Board in accordance with section 22. The Court held that insofar as lawyers, police officers and judicial officers are concerned, their position would be covered by implicitly including a defence. Since this was not necessary for purposes of the matter before the Court, the Court did not undertake such inclusion.

It is suggested that Parliament repeal the present definition (which was again amended in 2004 and 2009) of child pornography and replace it with the following definition: "child pornography" means any image, real or simulated, however created, explicitly depicting a person who is or who is shown as being under the age of 18 years (a) engaged in or participating in sexual conduct; (b) engaged in a display of genitals; or (c) assisting another person to

---

*   It would include a person older than 18 simulating the role of a child (so-called virtual pornography).

engage in sexual conduct which, judged within context, has as its predominant objective purpose the stimulation of sexual arousal, in contrast to aesthetic feeling, in its reasonable target audience and does not fall within the categories exempted in the Act.

This proposal includes the art, drama, science and documentary exemptions. The Constitutional Court did not do so explicitly, but it is clear from its judgment that all those exemptions would fall under aesthetic feelings. It would, accordingly, make good sense, if the definition simply included those exemptions. It is remarkable how close the definition of the Constitutional Court has come to the original definition as formulated by the 1994 Task Group. However, it is a more lenient definition than the original 1996 definition, since the material must be directed at creating sexual arousal. Parliament's 1999 intention to make the definition broader than the 1996 definition, was constitutionally clearly not acceptable. Unfortunately, the 2009 amendment excludes drama, science and art as defences in the case of child pornography. How anyone could believe that this exclusion is not unconstitutional remains a mystery to me. The Constitutional Court judgment is clear: drama, art and science would protect possession against prosecution. However, both the Independent Communications Authority of South Africa and the Broadcasting Complaints Commission have kept the defences intact in its 2009 Codes.

Remarkably, the Review Board, within the present 1996 Act, has in any case, given weight to dramatic merit in the light of the *De Reuck* judgment and overruled the Board in its rejection of an exemption to screen the film *XXY*, which deals with the problems of a boy who is heterosexual. Context was accentuated, in the light of the *De Reuck* judgment. All is, accordingly, not lost.[*]

The art exemption, *inter alia*, applies in the United States, Canada, the United Kingdom and Germany. For the United States, the Mapplethorpe trial in Cincinnati, Ohio illustrates the defence well. It concerned the exhibition of photographs of sexual abuse of children by Mapplethorpe, a renowned photographer. The exhibition took place in a special division of an

---

[*]   *Out in Africa: South African Gay and Lesbian Film Festival v Films and Publications Board* (case 1/2009).

art gallery and it was restricted to adults. Here the art exemption was apparently ("apparently" since it was a jury trial and no reasons were given; yet the jury could only have acquitted the manager of the museum as a result of art) applied.[*]

Section 163(6) of the Canadian Criminal Code includes the art defence. The Canadian Supreme Court's judgment in *Her Majesty the Queen v Sharpe*[†] attached special weight to artistic merit. The Court states that "the defence must be construed broadly".[‡]

Insofar as Germany is concerned, the *Strafgesetzbuch* §184(5) prohibits possession of pornographic material which has the abuse of children as subject. However, it is clear that the material must first also satisfy the requirement of pornography (between adults) as interpreted by the German Courts over many years. Scientific works are excluded from the term "pornography" whilst section 5 of the *Grundgesetz* protects art, except in the case of serious invasion into the rights of personality.

I SHOULD MAKE IT CLEAR THAT I AM ADAMANTLY against the involvement of children in the production of child pornography. However, the possession of the product may be excused when that product amounts to art or is included in a scientific study. If *Romeo and Juliet* were to be shown to have sex, as is the case in one of the modern film renditions, the drama or art exemption should exclude a finding by a court that the film includes child pornography. Of course, if the actors were indeed under 18, the producers would be liable to prosecution. These roles are, however, usually performed by young adults. In the recent film, *The Reader* (for which Kate Winslet won several awards as best actress, including a Bafta and an Oscar) the producers in fact waited until the boy, David Kross, was 18 before the film was shot. Of course, according to the Films and Publications Act, child pornography also includes instances where the person – although older than 18 – is shown to be under 18. Although I was the one who drafted the simulation of a person as under 18

---

[*]   Compare 1991 *Howard Law Journal* 339.

[†]   (2001) SCC 2 par [60].

[‡]   Paragraph [61].

into the 1996 Act, I believe that Parliament should remove the inclusion of simulation. It does not place a child at risk since a child is not truly involved. This was rightly done by the United States Supreme Court when it held the ban on virtual child pornography to be unconstitutional.* The drama exemption could save such scenes but, at present, the Films and Publications Act allows for no exemption. This is of course not compatible with the Constitution and the Constitutional Court judgment in the *De Reuck* case.†

Addendum Four: The Last Temptation of Christ

I would like to deal with some of the thoughts expressed in judging the Martin Scorcese film, *The Last Temptation of Christ*, at the Broadcasting Complaints Commission in 2007. In 1989, as chairman of the Publications Appeal Board, I wrote the judgment where the Board unanimously found the film to be offensive. In 2007 the constitutional paradigm had changed completely, and the BCCSA on appeal decided that etv had not contravened the Broadcasting Code by broadcasting the film after 23:00 with an age restriction of 18 and due classification. Here follows my current view on the film.

In the film the temptations put to Jesus in the Gospel is increased to include a last temptation: that of leading an ordinary life, including getting married and having a sexual relationship. This last temptation is, of course, not in accordance with the Gospel. Where Jesus is on the cross in the film, his mind wanders to what seems to be a momentary flight from his suffering, and the temptation to be married is placed before him. The author and producer add this last temptation in order to, as it were, complete the full circle. It is not simply plucked from the air, but builds on the doubt and uncertainty which Jesus, in the film, is seen to experience with regard to his task and his divine nature. He is confronted with the last temptation after he has uttered the words: "Father, why hast thou forsaken me!" Images of what his life might be like if he were not the Messiah then go through his mind: he

---

*   *Ashcroft v Free Speech Coalition et al.* 122 S.Ct.1389 (16 April 2002).

†   However, see the judgment of the Review Board in the *XXY* matter (above).

marries Mary Magdalene, and after she dies in childbirth, he weds Mary the sister of Lazarus and Martha. They have children. In one scene during this flight of imagination, it is implied that Jesus is seduced by Martha in the absence of Mary.

But the moment ends when Jesus's mental struggle ends and he is back on the cross. He then begs God to forgive him for having contemplated living an ordinary life – the last temptation. Therefore, once again, as was the case in regard to the temptations recorded in the Gospel, Jesus rejects this last temptation, which occurred during a momentary flight of imagination, believing that his Father had abandoned him. Having resisted the last temptation, He hangs on the cross and exclaims, "It is accomplished!"

The crucial question arises when Jesus is on the cross and Satan, masquerading as a guardian angel, puts the last temptation to Him and He, in a momentary flight of imagination, visualises what that life might be. It is this part of the film in particular that gave rise to the complaint at the BCCSA.

It must be acknowledged that the manner in which the film deals with the uncertainty that Jesus experiences at times regarding his divine purpose, is in conflict with the view of Christians.* The question is, however, whether it is not permissible for an author or film-maker to put the further question: may Jesus – as man – not have been tempted to get married? There are, of course, many ways in which this aspect could be misused sensationally by an author or producer. However, when the love scene is portrayed in the film there is nothing explicit about it. It is clear that, within the context of the film, Jesus visualised this last temptation whilst on the cross in a flight of imagination. He is shown to have overcome this last temptation in the same way as he rejected the other temptations. The end result is, accordingly, positive from

---

*   The first Tribunal's decision by my respected colleague, Prof. Henning Viljoen (with whom Prof. Sunette Lötter and Prof. Gerrit Olivier agreed) is available on the BCCSA website and deserves to be read (available at www.bccsa.co.za). The judgment on appeal, that found the broadcast not to have contravened the Broadcasting Code by Danie du Toit (with whom Prof. Wilhelm Jordaan, Prof. Willem de Klerk and Mr Ed Linington agreed) is also on the same website and also deserves to be read, since on the facts in the film it is found that Jesus, once again, did not give in to the "last" temptation.

an orthodox Christian perspective. The vision of the alternative life that Jesus may have lived is also fleeting. Of course, it lasts about 40 minutes in film time, but it is clear, when the scenes before and after the flight of imagination are compared, that the duration of the scenes depicting the alternative life was merely fleeting seconds.

I am not convinced that the protection of (religious) dignity is a permissible limitation to speech that is regarded as offensive on religious grounds. Section 16(2)(c) of the Constitution explicitly states that hate speech based on religion is not permitted. And that is the only limit to free speech in the case of religion. If the infringement of the right of dignity were to be the test, recourse would always be had to the right to dignity in complaints relating to hate speech, since the unlawful infringement of the right to dignity could be based on mere offensiveness, without a hate speech component. Where dignity is impaired, there could be compliance with the "harm" requirement in the hate speech definition. The infringement of the right to dignity alone is, however, not sufficient ground to impose a limitation on offensive religious speech. At the heart of freedom of religion lies the right to express views which could be offensive to adherents of the faith that is being criticised or attacked. Consequently, with respect, I do not agree with the approach in the Jamiat-Ul-Ulama (cartoons of the Prophet Mohammed) judgment in so far as the finding is based on the infringement of the right to dignity of adherents of the Islamic faith. It should be mentioned that the Court's order was on an application for an interim interdict and that the Court indicated that, in a full hearing, there would be an opportunity to flesh out the matter fully. However, although not fully discussed, the learned Judge does, nevertheless also find that there was an advocacy of hatred and, combined with the infringement of the right to dignity, the Court ultimately did base its conclusion on the advocacy of hatred plus the infringement of the right to dignity. This approach is, with respect, the correct approach.

The Last Temptation of Christ amounts to a dramatic work of quality – it is not a cartoon of Jesus. The film does not ridicule Jesus, but deals with the enormous burden that rested on Him as the Redeemer. The film is no cheap, vulgar exercise. It deals in a profound and dramatic manner with the spiritual struggle in the life of Jesus and, ultimately, with his victory in rejecting the temptation. On the whole, it has an overwhelming aesthetic impact on the reasonable viewer. As foreshadowed in the case of *De Reuck v Directorate of Public Prosecutions and Others,** the aesthetic dimension is paramount, therefore ensuring that the film remains within the bounds of the fundamental right of freedom of expression.

---

*   2004(1) SA 406(CC).